EFFECTIVE BUSINESS DECISION MAKING

...and the educated guess

William F. O'Dell

NTC Business Books
a division of NTC *Publishing Group* • Lincolnwood, Illinois USA

This book is dedicated to
my former students
at the McIntire School of Commerce of the University of Virginia
(who often wondered whether I knew what I was talking about)

Library of Congress Cataloging-in-Publication Data

O'Dell, William F. (William Francis), 1909–
    Effective business decision making and the educated guess /
William F. O'Dell.
        p.   cm.
    Includes bibliographical references and index.
    ISBN 0-8442-3289-0
    1. Decision-making.   I. Title.
HD30.23.027   1991
658.4'03—dc20   90-13489

Published by NTC Business Books, a division of NTC Publishing Group
4255 West Touhy Avenue, Lincolnwood (Chicago), Illinois 60646-1975 U.S.A.
© 1991 by NTC Publishing Group. All rights reserved.
No part of this book may be reproduced, stored in a retrieval system,
or transmitted in any form or by any means,
electronic, mechanical, photocopying, recording or otherwise,
without the prior permission of NTC Publishing Group.
Manufactured in the United States of America.
1 2 3 4 5 6 7 8 9 BC 9 8 7 6 5 4 3 2 1

Here's what the experts are saying about *Effective Business Decision Making:*

"Bill O'Dell has presented decision making as an understandable, satisfying, and rewarding activity. This book redirects our focus to thinking about the orderly and efficient use of information rather than merely the processing of data." *R.H. Matzke, President, Chevron Overseas Petroleum, Inc.*

"A real problem in business today is making effective decisions without drowning in all of the data. Bill O'Dell puts forth a very helpful, easy-to-grasp model. This is a book you'll both enjoy and benefit from—written by a pro." *William J. Peters, Former Dean, The Koged College of Business Administration, The American University, Washington, D.C.*

"This book helps light the path to clear decisions, while spotting the many misleading signals along the way . . . If there were a perfect system, we'd all use it and all be successful. Bill O'Dell's decision-making process can increase the odds in your favor." *George Gruenwald, Corporate Growth and Development Consultant, Former CEO, Campbell-Mithun Inc.*

"Bill O'Dell shows how a member of a group can arrive at a good decision in any problem situation and in the process persuade others to reach the same conclusion on their own. Even if one sees no need for doing this to others, it is useful to know when others may be doing this to you." *Dr. George Brown, Former Director of Marketing Research, Ford Motor Company*

CONTENTS

FOREWORD

Bill O'Dell was my first boss and my best teacher.

First of all, Bill knows that getting an organization to make *and* implement good business decisions starts with the *right attitude* of the boss towards his colleagues. Colleagues who are fearful, suspicious, or angry rarely make or implement good decisions. Bill knows how to make business colleagues feel good about themselves, their ideas, and their colleagues.

Second, Bill knows that life—and business—is a choice among alternatives. By teaching me to focus on a number of alternatives—and their pluses and minuses in terms of one's articulated goals, he stretched my mind beyond the linear and ossifying focus on ''the one and only''—in other words, my alternative.

Finally, Bill knows that humor can often make the point far better, while leaving far fewer scars.

Because I have always felt that the best management development was having a good boss—and I never had a better one—I am absolutely delighted to recommend this book.

> Peter G. Peterson
> Former U.S. Secretary of Commerce
> Chairman, The Blackstone Group L.P.

WHY THIS BOOK?

The age of information
Is now at hand;
But the more I know
The less I understand.

Bruce Kafaroff

There you have it, in a nutshell. Information—and how to deal with it—is what this book is all about. It has been written to help you understand and apply information in every decision you make.

In today's business world, information abounds. We are inundated. We struggle with the masses of data thrown in our direction, hour after hour, day after day. Data overload. We scan it, we study it, we analyze it, we review it. We know that information holds the answers to our business questions, but we can't find them. We are lost.

In business, information is sometimes loftily called a ''strategic corporate asset'' and the ''key to global competitiveness.'' But no matter how highly we prize information, until we learn how to manage it to our advantage, it is of no use to us. It is effective use of information that separates success from failure, and winning decisions from disastrous ones. Understand how to apply the multitudes of data your organization abounds in, and you will stay miles ahead of your competition.

Few people realize the connection between the information around them and the decisions they make. Virtually all information ultimately leads to a decision—not necessarily an immediate decision or an even good one, but a decision down the road just the same. To be a successful decision maker, then, is to take control of the sometimes overwhelming deluge of information around you.

When you make a decision, the consequences are there for all to see: your boss, your peers, the shareholders, the public, the competition, the government. Your decision making affects both your organization and your industry. Too many wrong decisions and you'll not only damage your business, you're likely to lose your position. Someone just in back of you is ready to step forward. Understanding decision making is a vital part of business life, and it can make or break individual careers.

Effective Business Decision Making is an easy-to-read, down-to-earth guide to becoming a better decision maker. It will help you understand how people and information interact during decision making. In non-technical language, this slender volume explains exactly what happens during what we will call the decision-making process. You will learn how to gather and apply information relevant to each decision you make and how to present this persuasively to others. As most business decisions are made by groups of people rather than by individuals, the focus is on consensus decision making. The book will help you improve your ability to communicate with and enlist the support of others—both skills which are essential in reaching final, consensus decisions.

But there are times when all the information available to you will not be enough—when you must go it alone. Numbers will not substitute for your "educated guess." This can happen several times during the decision-making process, and this book alerts you to these situations—predicaments in which you find you must rely on your judgment, regardless of how much information you have.

The book was written after a lifetime of exposure to decisions made in all walks of industry—from the large automobile manufacturers and food processors, to the local retail store. I have had a close-up view of highly successful decisions made by brilliant men and women. I have also observed disastrous choices by equally brilliant men and women. Why did some of their decisions succeed and others misfire? Because, in many instances, the decision makers simply did not understand how decision making works.

The reader in business will find this book helpful in many specific ways, but primarily in making himself or herself a better decision maker within the organization. It follows, then, that this achievement will lead to enhanced job satisfaction, greater recognition, and higher income.

•••

Acknowledgments

As every author knows, listing acknowledgments is risky simply because there is always the chance of omitting someone who has made an important contribution. However, I can without hesitation single out two persons who have aided considerably in developing this final product. David K. Hardin, a long-time friend who knows the information business as well as anybody, contributed ideas and items. Andrew C. Ruppel, my long-time colleague at the McIntire School of Commerce at the University of Virginia, gave freely of his time, making certain that I did not get too far out of line. His counsel was invaluable.

Reflected also on the pages of this book are the thoughts of Mr. Ruppel, Robert H. Trent, and William J. Kehoe, my co-authors of *Marketing Decision Making: Analytic Framework and Cases,* published by South-Western Publishing Company.

A special paragraph must be reserved for Anne Knudsen, associate editor of NTC Business Books. Anne combines her delightful amiability derived from her years in England with an exceptional talent as an editor.

Summary Flowchart

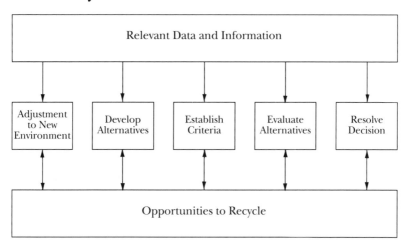

1

WHAT DOES CONSENSUS DECISION MAKING INVOLVE?

You and Decision Making

You are on your way to work, walking along the sidewalk about two blocks from your office. As you approach an intersection, you see the traffic light turn from green to amber. You are a few feet from the curb. You glance quickly to your right, see a car advancing, and decide that with a mild burst of speed you can cross the street well ahead of the car, whose driver barely slackens speed.

Changing your pace from a walk to a run provided you with ample margin of safety, although had you tripped and fallen you could have encountered serious, even fatal, injury. But you did not relish losing those few moments waiting for the green light and knew that a quickened pace would reduce to near zero any risk of being hit. It was this information—gained through viewing the advancing car—that made you decide to cross on the amber.

This is a simple example of decision making. Let's analyze it more closely to find out exactly what takes place during what we will call in this book, the decision making process (DMP). Within seconds you posed two alternatives: wait for the green light, or cross on the amber. Observing the oncoming car gave you sufficient information to aid you in opting for the second. The consequences of a wrong decision were great—you could have been killed—but your information was such that the probabilities against this were heavily in your favor.

As your day progresses you will make decisions even more quickly than this. Many will stem from instinct or impulse. Even though we like to think of ourselves as rational animals, basing decisions on logic, reason, and objective criteria, the fact is that often our egos, insecurities, and tastes dictate the actions we take. This is true of both personal decisions, and those we make on behalf of our company or institution.

Behavioral scientists have developed sophisticated terms describing how decisions are made, but through it all—whether your decisions are personal or organizational—they are to a great extent sparked by the non-rational. And because of this, the decisions you make are not without risk. You could marry the wrong person, and risk the tremendous penalty of unhappiness. Or, upon graduating from high school, you could decide prematurely on a career as a brain surgeon. This might be great for your ego in the short term, but you might later realize it was the wrong decision for you. Again, the result is unhappiness.

This book will help you reduce the risks involved in making decisions. It is aimed at the business decision maker who strives to achieve a rational approach to selecting the ''best'' courses of action for his or her organization. This is called ''rational decision making,'' or the ''scientific method.'' The decisions may be made individually by you, or jointly in participation with a group of people, such as a committee within your organization. In either case, you are a decision maker. Whatever your role or level of responsibility, you need to understand decision making and its importance in business life. That is what this book is about.

Know Yourself through Decision Making

Remember the old joke about the woman working on a potato-processing line? Her job was to sort the potatoes coming down the conveyer belt at the rate of a dozen or so a minute into three sizes: large, medium, and small. After work one evening, she was asked how her day went. Her obvious reply: ''Decisions, decisions, decisions.'' If you don't think this joke is funny, you can laugh at its age.

The level of the decisions *you* make within your organization can give you a meaningful clue on how ''successful'' you are. If, like the potato-sorting lady's, your decisions have no great impact on the firm's performance or profitability, you are on a low rung of the hierarchical ladder. On the other hand, if you alone or jointly resolve issues that profoundly affect your organization's future, you have progressed well, at least within the structure of your company.

Another way to relate decisions to your own progress is to assess them in terms of whether you are mostly concerned with how well you *personally* are doing, or how well your organization *as a whole* is performing. Are you primarily worried about yourself and your job? Or, do your interests center on the future welfare of your company within its industry? In the context of decision making, is your chief desire to look good within the company? Or, is your goal to make decisions that strengthen the company's position? Taken one step further, does your decision making pertain to your industry's growth and destiny, thus enhancing your company's own position and growth?

Step back and look at your decision-making role. This will tell you a lot about where you stand in terms of your organization, and in terms of your career.

· ·

Individual vs. Consensus Decisions

A key difference between personal decisions and the decisions you make on behalf of your organization is that organizational decisions are rarely made alone. They are made by consensus.

Of course, there are times when you as a decision maker within the organization act as a loner, and take action without consulting or communicating with anyone else. But the more important the decision, the less likely it is that you will be on your own. The vast majority of business decisions are made in conjunction with others. Even the widely heralded, Hollywood-type hard-nosed executive, barking out directives in rapid-fire fashion is a rare bird indeed.

Perhaps you are a member of a group engaged in decision making, such as a finance committee that needs to decide how to reduce the cost of acquiring capital. Or, you may be part of the company's product development committee, seeking approval for a new product. You could, of course, be the head of one or more company committees. Regardless of your role or level of responsibility, seldom do you find yourself making decisions entirely on your own. Even on simple, everyday matters, you are likely to converse with your boss or colleagues.

Business decisions are, therefore, made by groups, acting together for the good of the company. And, of course, groups are made up of people— all with different interests, views, responsibilities, and opinions. Understanding people and communicating successfully with them is central to effective decision making.

Human behavior can be erratic, unpredictable, and ruled by emotions. The more people involved—and the more egos at play—the more complex the decision-making process becomes. Let's look at an example, to see how difficult and how emotive group decision making can be.

You crossed the street safely and arrived at your office. A meeting is in progress at which a final decision is to be made regarding whether to commercialize nationally your firm's newly-developed Special Product KR. The meeting has been called by the financial vice-president, Mr. F Participating are the production vice-president, Ms. P, the marketing vice-president, Mr. M, yourself (a product manager), and your assistant. Mr. F's memo announcing the meeting stated that the purpose was to make a decision on whether to market the new product on a national scale. Special Product KR has been tested on a rather sophisticated but limited basis, and the test data have been dispersed to all persons attending the meeting.

Mr. F opens with a review of the test data, following it with a statement on the financial risks of more than $3 million in "going national." He asserts that he is opposed to national or even regional distribution of the product. In short, he says, "Let's forget Special Product KR. It won't make it."

Mr. M takes a somewhat softer position, urging that more test data be obtained. Ms. P, on the other hand, confuses the issue by talking about reducing packaging costs, saying that if the product is to be tested further, she would like to use a redesigned box for the test.

The meeting goes on and on. It gets late and little real progress has been made. The fact is, there seems to be some regression, and tempers are now flaring and accusations are being made.

Except for your assistant, you are the youngest and least experienced person in the room. You are not about to tell these vice presidents how to do their jobs. However, you do know why they are failing to make progress. They are all talking about different issues—they are all at different stages in the decision-making process. There is little or no chance of reaching a meaningful decision unless they get back on track and talk about one issue at a time. You make one attempt to bring some semblance of order to the discussion, but so tense is the climate by now that you are told in no uncertain terms to back off.

The problem here is that the members of this group do not understand what is involved in consensus decision making. Instead of progress toward a decision, the meeting results in maximum frustration and minimum productivity. Two important elements were missing: the basic issue to be resolved was not stated in clear terms and recognized by everyone; and the discussion was not led by reason or rational thinking. As often happens in group decision making, opinions, emotions, and instincts were allowed to take over.

This is just one of the criticisms most frequently leveled against group meetings. The committee approach has been denigrated by many. One often hears how companies ''governed by committees'' are slow to act or respond to change. To gather people into a room, to review what has transpired at previous meetings for those who were unable to attend, to discuss and disagree the points at issue, to restrain aggressive members from dominating the meeting—all this is time consuming and cumbersome.

With all its faults, however, consensus decision making is pretty much the way of life in any company or organization. It is difficult to make other than the most minor decisions alone. Most individuals lack the expertise in each area of the business that a major decision would require. Moreover, groups are almost always more creative than loners. In any search for alternative ways to do things, group interaction is the best way to develop a large number of well-informed, varied, and creative options. The reasons? More information, based on different experiences and expertise, is assembled. Judgments are compared and combined.

Moreover, once a committee decision is made and approved by all involved, there is an open commitment to moving forward and implementing the action decided on. All members have an interest in seeing the consensus decision work, and will be motivated to help and to monitor its execution.

For all of these reasons, the committee or group approach is the best way to handle major decisions. It is, however, essential that each member participates, and that issues are approached with logic and reason. Let's look at some ways in which this can be achieved.

· ·

Getting Along with and Persuading Others

Dale Carnegie, best-selling author of self-help books, makes an important connection between the ability to get along with others and the ability to persuade. These are two skills that are central to participating effectively in business meetings.

The basic challenge in any committee or group meeting is to make certain that the members of the group get along and can communicate well with each other. In group meetings, everyone's opinion and ideas count, no matter how high or how low each person is on the company hierarchy. The dominating, long-time company executive, for example, justifies his or her opinions, largely because of lengthy tenure with the firm. But, at the other extreme, the young committee member, more knowledgeable but insecure, may hesitate to voice suggestions. The trick to holding an effective meeting is to understand and manage different personalities so that every voice can be heard.

Long-term employees are often hardest to handle. They value reputation, experience, and length of service above all else, and egos and opinions can be unyielding. Even when they know they may be on shaky ground, long-term employees often don't like to give in. Less-experienced employees, too, reveal their insecurities in group meetings, and are often highly influenced by a desire to look good in front of others, especially the boss.

Getting along with other committee members is vital to the decision-making process. Improper people-handling causes unnecessary delays and friction, and on occasion can result in the wrong decisions being made.

"One thing about Martin, he doesn't mince words."

Drawing by Modell; © 1985 The New Yorker Magazine, Inc.

Linked with this ability to get along, is the skill of persuading others. Good powers of persuasion can direct and smooth the progress of any meeting. There are a few simple rules to follow if you want to improve your skills in influencing others. Let's look at some of these.

The first is, *do not minimize the views of the person you are confronting.* It is much better to enhance the ego of a person whose opinion differs from yours than to confront that person openly. The more important the issue to be resolved, the greater the need to handle the other person with kid gloves. Compliment your "opponent" on the depth of thought associated with the view presented. Give credit for the opinion expressed and the arguments used. State that you readily understand why such a position is being propounded. Belabor this, when appropriate, even to the point that your opponent begins to feel that you agree. Then, gradually and tactfully, move on to express your opinion. You can suggest modestly that you would like to present "a thought that could have some merit," or a viewpoint that "perhaps is worth consideration."

A second simple rule is: *take your time in disagreeing.* Never respond to a committee member with statements like "I don't agree!" or, worse still, "You're wrong!" This, obviously, will only raise that person's emotions to the point of anger, and he or she will then be defensive to the bitter end. An expert in handling people will sometimes let an entire meeting conclude on a thought with which he or she disagrees, only to come into the next session and voice a contrary point of view. This approach is effective when one view—to the exclusion of others—is strongly argued in a meeting. It takes skill and time to alter strongly-held opinions.

Another technique that can work wonders on less major issues is the "ten second ceiling" approach. Suppose that in the meeting someone expresses a point of view. You hold a contrary opinion. Before you state your position, it is important to communicate to your opponent that you respect his or her view and you are not rejecting it outright. If you do this successfully, your opponent will then show more patience and respect in listening to your ideas. So before you respond, look at the ceiling for ten seconds. This gives the impression that you are stopping to think seriously about that person's argument before you answer. Then, go ahead and present your opinion.

People are essential to decision making, but because of their individualistic and often "peculiar" behavior, they can create obstacles that lead to incorrect actions. Understanding and dealing with people is as vital as the decision-making process itself. Remember this as you read the chapters that follow.

2

WHAT IS THE DECISION-MAKING PROCESS?

In the opening chapter, we mentioned in loose terms the decision-making process (DMP). This chapter will focus on explaining exactly what elements are involved in making effective decisions. We will show you how a thorough understanding of the DMP can make you a better business decision maker.

A good grounding in the DMP can profoundly influence both your business and personal life. You will discover a new dimension in the world about you. It will appear more orderly. Your meetings will be more productive, less time consuming. Your relations with others will take on a more comfortable pattern. Topping it all, of course, is the fact that you will be making better decisions or, at least, participating more fully in the making of these decisions. The results are obvious. You will look better in the eyes of your superiors. You will progress more rapidly within your organization. You will make more money. Understanding the decision-making process can also save you from making mistakes. It could even save you from being fired, for, as we all know, poor decisions and job security are seldom compatible. Just pick up any issue of *The Wall Street Journal* or *Business Week* and read about the latest top executives who lost their jobs because they failed to make the right decisions. In short, finding out about the decision-making process becomes one of the most important business moves you can make.

Different Approaches to Decision Making

The decision-making process (DMP) is a means by which you can take control of the many, variant factors that making decisions involves. You will learn how to recognize the different elements of decision making, and how to know, at each stage, exactly where you are along the path. Many are the times when you have been in meetings, like the one described in the previous chapter, where the chairperson allows participants to wander off on tangents from the central issue. This occurs simply because the leader does not recognize the guideposts that impart where the members of the meeting are—and where they should be—in resolving that issue. At the outset, then, to keep people on track it is essential to know what is really taking place when a decision is in the making.

For years, the academic world and others have studied what happens during decision making and have suggested techniques through which business people can improve their skills. Prevalent in recent years has been the highly-touted "case study approach," used in almost all graduate schools of business and management. This method involves setting up in the classroom a simulation of the business environment in which participants "solve" a business problem. Prior to the meeting, students study voluminous fact sheets, detailing aspects of an organization's operations, including data on such functions as finance, marketing, production, and so on. The professor opens with a vague "What's the problem?" or "What's your interpretation of today's case?" No clear objective is set and an open-ended discussion ensues.

The obvious flaw with this approach is that it does not take into account the influences at large in the real business world. It is static, and does not allow for changes in the environment in which the organization operates. For example, in most real business situations, lack of vital information is a good reason for delaying a decision. Meetings are postponed until new or better information is obtained. This isn't an option in the classroom, and so students get into a habit of narrowing their perspectives and make decisions based on misleading or missing information.

I have, as an observer, sat through a good number of case discussions in graduate business schools, including Harvard. I am impressed with these graduate schools' and professors' failure to develop decisional objectives for the cases being deliberated. I have listened to professors "overintellectualize" cases at the close of the sessions, sometimes with conclusions opposed to those I would have come up with. This is not to say that one person is right and the other wrong. When you have a case so openended in its evidence, anyone can argue with a high degree of plausibility in support of several possible conclusions. The problem, then, may not be so much with the case method as with the quality and nature of the cases used. Students are left directionless in most case discussions—swimming in the swamp, so to speak.

A second problem with the case study approach is the lack of decisional direction. The professor may nudge students with such deliberately ambiguous questions as "Do you really believe that?" Or, "Do you understand the problem?" Or the completely formless, "Why?" No real direction is given and no objectives are set. This means that although students may be exposed to a great deal of data on a particular organization, they are not moving toward a decision. Discussions wander because students do not understand that decision making is a process, and to be successful it must move along a given course. Case studies do not show them where they are in the process or where to go.

This approach, then, is ineffective as a decision-making tool because of its hypothetical nature, its open-endedness, and its lack of direction. At the other end of the extreme are the highly structured approaches to decision making that have over the years been offered by the academe and others.

A structured approach usually presents decision making as a system involving four or five rigidly ordered "steps." They go something like this:

1. Define the problem

2. State the hypothesis

3. Gather the facts

4. Examine the consequences

5. Make the decision

These steps, stated without explanation and in the order dictated here, are quite meaningless. First off, what *is* a problem? I tend to dislike the term when discussing decision making. It is so vague that seldom will two people interpret it in the same way. Sure, a problem represents something that has a degree of uncertainty, something to be "solved." But no one likes problems. The word implies trouble and difficulty. It is negative. Let's use the word "decision" instead. It implies a much more positive approach to setting a course for action.

Step 2, state the hypothesis, has strong academic overtones. The fact is, most business people do not think in terms of hypotheses. The hard-headed business person who has never taken a course in formal logic does not want to hear about hypothetical situations, and is, instead, more interested in the "real thing."

Let's move on to Step 3, gather the facts. What facts? How do you "gather facts?" And Step 4, examine the consequences. What does that mean? What consequences are we talking about? Thus, with such meager help from Steps 1 to 4, Step 5, make the decision, is practically impossible.

In real life—in the hard and demanding world of business—the components that lead to an effective decision are not neatly formed, highly-structured, or well-ordered in this "lock-step" fashion. Decisions are—as we saw in Chapter 1—made by people, and for that reason the various stages will almost invariably overlap. People are unpredictable, situations change. This is why decision making rarely follows a smooth and clearly-defined path. There are jerks and jumps, we respond to changes, we re-trace our steps, and we move forward again. This may happen several times before we finally come to the decision itself, the course of action. Let us not restrict ourselves to the notion that decision making can be approached step by step. Quite the opposite is true. It is made up of different and inter-related phases or stages, all recognizable if you understand the processes behind them.

Decision making is not an abstract or "textbook" exercise. It involves real people who can influence, control, or complicate it. In the pages that follow you will not find any lengthy case studies based on assumptions that would not be acceptable in the real world. You will not find sets of neat instructions to take you directly from *a* to *b*. What you will find is a view of the processes involved in decision making that are practiced every day by individuals on behalf of their organizations in a competitive and changing business environment.

A Model for Decision Making

The first thing to remember is that the path to every decision has a beginning, a middle, and an end. Understanding how decision making works requires that you have a ready grasp of the complete framework that embraces this entire process, from start to finish. We will call this framework the DMP model. Once you master this, you will be able to determine, at all times, exactly where you are in the decision-making process. And, just as important, you will be aware of where others in your group are within the same process. Understanding and using the model in all the decisions you make will help you keep discussions on track, communicate your ideas, reduce wasted time, boost the overall productivity of your group, and earn the appreciation and respect of your colleagues.

First, then, what is a DMP model? It is a simplified version of a complex set of happenings that take place on the road to a course of action. The model exhibits the main elements that influence any decision and reveals how they overlap and interrelate. It is a miniature, simplified version of the real thing—the path toward a decision.

The DMP model is far from a rigid structure. Instead, it is flexible and malleable, capable of adjusting to changes in the business environment, and to the decision makers' assumptions and agreements. Any decision will fit on this model, be it complex or simple, strategic or tactical, of little consequence or of great significance. It can be used to handle both qualitative and quantitative information. At the beginning of the decision making process you can place the attitudes and opinions of your group or committee on the model. Later, as you move along the road to final action, you will (but not always) work with numbers, or quantitative data, as you reach the analytic elements of the decision. All the time, numbers or not, you are fitting the movements and attitudes of the decision makers onto your decision model.

Elements of the DMP Model

The major elements of the model are summarized below. This serves as an overview of the ground we will cover in the rest of the book.

Again, keep in mind that every decision has a beginning, a middle, and an end. Within this framework, there are five phases or stages—not necessarily consecutive—through which decisions proceed. Using this formula to understand the decisions you are making will increase your chances of proceeding in the right direction.

Phase 1: Recognizing the New Environment.

The genesis of a business decision takes place within a specific business environment, such as, for example, the financial, production, marketing, personnel, or purchasing department within the organization, or the national or international setting in which the industry operates. The need for a decision is sparked when someone recognizes that an event has taken place or a situation exists that suggests an adjustment should be made if the organization is to perform well in this newly-created or newly recognized environment. *Recognizing the possible need to adjust to a new or newly-discovered environment is the beginning of a decision.*

Phase 2: Developing Alternatives.

Stating the possible options to be considered for adjusting successfully to the new environment appears, at first, to be a simple assignment. Beware! It is demanding, and the wrong choices can be perilous. So your sales have declined—what are the options you should consider? Increased advertising? A change in price? Drop the product from the line? Or what? The options are varied and each should be examined carefully.

Phase 3: Establishing Criteria.

On what basis will the "best" alternative be selected? "Best" according to what standard? Profit? Market share? Return on investment? Again, there are a number of possibilities. Establishing criteria and ensuring that each person involved understands them enables the decision makers to set forth the basis for choosing one option over the others.

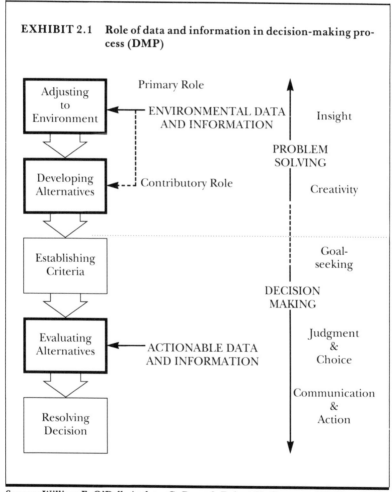

EXHIBIT 2.1   Role of data and information in decision-making process (DMP)

Source: William F. O'Dell, Andrew C. Ruppel, Robert H. Trent, and William J. Kehoe, *Marketing Decision Making,* Fourth Edition, South-Western Publishing Co., Cincinnati, 1988, p. 31

Phase 4: Evaluating Alternatives.

The decision makers assess the options in light of pre-determined criteria and, with or without additional data or information, attempt to choose the one option that best satisfies the criteria. This is largely where the "rational," purely quantitative factors come into play. If disagreement emerges, this is a sign that the selection of an option should be delayed and additional information or expert opinion obtained.

Phase 5: Implementing the Decision.

With or without additional information, a final course of action is selected and put into operation. Thus, a new environment is formed.

Of course, all decisions do not follow identical paths. Rarely do they progress smoothly from Phase 1 to Phase 5. A decision maker may jump from Phase 2 to Phase 5 so quickly that the interim phases are not mentioned or touched upon in any way. They may be so obvious that they are glossed over or implied. But, remember, they are still there. In other instances, the sequential movement from phase to phase may grind to a halt, reverse itself, retrace earlier ground, encounter dead ends, and finally proceed to the final decision. The decision makers can go around in circles, as new data become available or situations change.

You can see from the model, too, that once a decision has been made, a new one is in the making. Let's say you have decided to reduce the price of one item in your product line. Things begin to happen. Your sales increase. Your competition meets the price. Thus, a new environment is born, and a subsequent decision is necessary.

You will also realize that each major decision that culminates in a final course of action is made up of any number of "mini-decisions." Any one business decision may depend on the outcomes of a dozen or more decisions made en route. Each decision is peppered throughout with smaller choices or "wheels-within-a-wheel" to be resolved. And all of these mini-decisions are themselves candidates for the five-phase DMP model.

Decision making is dynamic, not static. It doesn't really matter whether you think of the DMP as linear or circular. What *is* important is that you visualize each decision as the creator of a new environment and, as we shall see later, act accordingly.

In the chapters which follow, we will examine closely the five phases of the DMP model.

3

A Decision's Beginning: The Environment

C ompanies striving for growth and fair returns on investment live in turbulent environments. Unhappy customers, unpredictable suppliers, and aggressive competition create uncertainties galore. Add to these the sometimes sudden changes in tax rulings, government regulations, labor demands, the intricacies of the economy, and the domestic and world political climates, and you have a business environment that is beset with change, uncertainty, and risk.

You and your firm are not alone. Your competitors face the same changing situations. What sets you, as a successful organization, apart from the others is the skill with which you cope with the constant and often punishing changes that disrupt the environment in which your company operates.

But neither you, your firm, nor your competitors can control that environment. You may influence it, at times, in some small way, but even this is unusual. Whether in personal or business life, the best you can do is make sure you are aware of what is happening in the world around you and adjust to the changes it brings. If, for example, you buy bonds for a financial house, you keep a careful eye on the credit markets. A change in interest rates could cause you to revise your purchasing plans. Or, let's say you are the programming director for a TV network or cable channel. You watch the Nielson ratings with avid interest because a drop in viewership for one of your shows means that you should take some action. No matter what your business, keeping a close eye on the environment in which you operate can mean the difference between success and failure. You must filter out and predict the probable effects of events or situations that could impact you, your product, your company, or your industry.

In recent years, too, the rapid advances in technology—particularly information technology—mean that the ability to respond to change is increasingly important to business survival. In today's business world, transmission of information is almost instantaneous. An event that occurs halfway around the world is on our television screens within hours, and even minutes. The personal computer and data processing revolution, with networks expanding worldwide, has provided another electronic highway for the acquisition and diffusion of information. The challenge for business is to absorb from the flood of numbers and data that bombard us from all sides the information we need. To stay in control we need to isolate and understand those factors that influence our performance and on which we can take action. Learning how to identify and adjust to new or newly-changed environments is the starting point in the decision-making process.

Recognizing New or Changed Environments

I have a hunch I was present some years ago during the meeting at which the genesis of the decision to develop Ford's Mustang automobile emerged. I had taken part in a study conducted for Ford by Chicago-based marketing research firm, Market Facts, Inc. Among the data gathered were figures on the resale value of a wide range of automobile makes and year models. One finding was the unexpectedly high resale price tag of early Thunderbirds. Further research revealed that the car appealed most to a consumer group dominated by single men in their twenties. John A. Frechtling of Ford's marketing research department mused, ''Why don't we build a car to appeal to this market segment?'' Ford did. The successful Ford Mustang resulted.

The point of the story is this. Research revealed a newly-discovered environment. Ford recognized it. From here, the decision was made to adjust to it by creating the Mustang.

Recognizing changes or situations in the environment that reveal a need for adjustment is where successful decision making starts. You can enhance your skills in spotting these through understanding the different factors that influence the business environment. These factors can be classified into three broad types: those that threaten current business performance, those that deviate from expected patterns of performance, and those that ''lurk'' beneath the surface and which, if discovered, can improve performance. In the rest of this book, we will refer to these as the Threat, the Deviation from the Expected, and the Lurking Situation. Let's look at each in turn.

The Threat

A threatening situation that affects the business environment is one which comes into being as a result of events caused by the actions of others, of people or organizations over whom or over which you have no control.

Competitors are often the culprits. Like you, they deliberately keep a tight lid on their plans, thus increasing the ''lead time'' before other organizations can catch up and respond to their actions. When a competitor, for example, unexpectedly drops its list price on certain products within a line, the first thing you and your firm will do is contemplate what action, if any, might be taken in response. There is an immediate need to adjust to the threat. Similarly, when Mars raises—rather than lowers—prices on its candy bars, Hershey is faced with a new environmental situation that just as certainly dictates that some reaction be considered.

The Threat, however, is not necessarily one that is unexpected. For example, when IBM introduced its personal computer in 1981, you can be sure this did not catch the management at Apple by surprise. But even though Apple saw it coming, it was a perturbing and potentially threatening event. The Threat created a new market environment to which Apple needed to respond. Apple was ready. The firm ran full page advertisements in newspapers around the country welcoming IBM to the world of personal computers. Apple stressed its delight that IBM was joining the field, insisting that the move would in the end expand the total market. Apple was right.

It is not only actions by the competition that can pose threats to the stability of the business environment. Government at any level—federal, state, county, city, school, sanitary district, transportation, zoning—constantly instigates changes that disrupt the ways businesses operate. Let's look at some examples.

In the early 1980s the drug manufacturer Eli Lilly and Company introduced an anti-arthritic prescription drug called Oraflex. The company had filed the required New Drug Application with the Food and Drug Administration (FDA), and the drug was subsequently approved for distribution. Later, the FDA accused Lilly of withholding information on the side effects of Oraflex and, after a series of exchanges, Lilly decided to withdraw the drug from the market, even though the company maintained it was safe and effective when used as directed. Lilly had initially predicted a $100 million profit on first-year sales, but instead had to take a $11.4 million write-down for Oraflex losses. Never mind who was right or wrong, the result was that a change in the environment caused by the FDA's actions severely threatened both the product line and the company's future policies. Lilly had to adjust to the new situation and decide what possible actions—if any—it should consider.

Outside suppliers, too, can threaten business operations. For example, suppose a supplier finds itself with a strike on its hands and, as a result, you face a short supply of needed parts. Your production declines. You may need to lay off some employees. Your customers go elsewhere. A myriad of threatening environmental circumstances arises and a series of adjustments has to be made if you are to survive. The Threat, posed by the supplier's problem, is the beginning of a chain of decisions for you.

Threatening situations are not necessarily restricted to individual companies. They can affect all organizations within a particular industry. Look, for example, at what happened in the machine tool industry in the 1980s. Within a two-year span, the industry output dropped from better than $5 billion to almost $2 billion. About one fourth of the companies, including major manufacturers, went out of business. To counteract foreign competition, which had contributed significantly to the decline of the domestic industry, industry leaders urged that higher duties be placed on imported machines. The word out of Washington, however, was that little help along these lines would be forthcoming. Increased foreign competition and the government's failure to take action constituted an industry-wide environment that was threatening and that required action. The decisions made by each company to respond to the Threat would result in their recovery or their further decline.

The examples show that decisions are set in motion when threatening events affect your firm, your product or service, or your industry. Hershey, Apple, Eli Lilly, and the machine tool industry were all exposed to threatening environments, brought about by circumstances beyond the organization's control. Each event is a threat not only because it calls for a response, but because of the likely negative responses of failing to adjust.

The Deviation from the Expected

How pleasant it is to know that everything is proceeding exactly as planned. You introduce a new product and its sales reach the predicted levels. You speed up the production line and productivity goes up correspondingly. Your employees as a whole are not unhappy about the change. All is as you forecast. One can easily argue that as long as everything proceeds as anticipated, there is no need for new management decisions. But, as we all know, the ''norm'' is rarely the case, and the unexpected often happens. Your company introduces a new product and its sales are well below predictions. Production costs, too, are higher than you anticipated, and personnel turnover is faster. The economy moves up—or down—more than forecast by your economists, and this, too, affects your production levels. Any one of these situations that deviate from the expected, and worlds of others, creates new environments to which you must adjust in order to survive and grow. *Management by exception,* as it is termed, becomes the norm.

How can you recognize when a Deviation from the Expected occurs? There are often tell-tale signs within your organization. The data contained in your financial statements are, for example, an excellent starting point. Let's say your profits for the month are down when you had anticipated an increase. This is certainly a deviation from expected patterns of performance, but all you know at this point is that something has not worked out as planned. What caused that decline in profits? Further analysis is required to turn financial data into a meaningful interpretation of the environment.

A loss or a drop in profit could be occasioned by any one or more of a number of factors: product/merchandise failure, over- or under-pricing, ineffective advertising, inadequate distribution, poor sales effort, competitive actions, narrow retail margins, supplier failure, and many others. It is often difficult to pinpoint the cause or causes from financial data alone, but some reasonably sophisticated data analysis can at least relate certain activities or situations to the revenue decline or cost increase.

A simple example. Your computerized data reveal that your sales costs are up appreciably. This is interesting news, but unless you go a step further and look at costs incurred in specific sales territories or by individual representatives, you will not know what adjustments you need to make. Let's say you inspect sales costs of individual representatives over the last six months. Six months ago, ten percent of staff accounted for 15 percent of sales costs. These same representatives now account for 40 percent of costs. You may still not have all the information you need to make a decision and take action, but at least you know where to start.

In summary, tracking the reasons for a Deviation from the Expected will tell you a great deal about your business environment and will give you clues on factors that should be considered when adjusting to these new situations.

The Lurking Situation

With both the Threat and the Deviation from the Expected, signs that a decision is necessary are usually immediately evident or can easily be discovered. You recognize these situations without trying. They hit you hard and cannot be avoided. Often, however, it is not immediately obvious that the environment has changed or is changing. Factors that influence it lie in wait or lurk beneath the surface. These "lurking" situations are the ones that only the most astute organizations will discover. As well as indicating the need for change, it is hidden situations that most often offer new opportunities. Learn how to discover from the environment factors that can be related to or that can influence your industry or organization, and you will find new opportunities that will give you an edge over your competition.

To illustrate environmental factors that lurk beneath the surface, let's look at some examples of situations which businesses have recognized and from which they have developed new opportunities.

Heavy snowfalls of near-catastrophic proportions inundate many U.S. cities and counties each year. It is difficult to predict where and when they will occur. Snow removal costs far exceed the budgets of the local authorities responsible for clearing snow. Assume you are with an insurance company. How would you interpret this information to uncover new opportunities for your organization? The National Union Fire Insurance Company of Pittsburgh, a member of the American National Group, created its "catastrophic snow budget stabilization insurance." The company recognized an environment in which unpredictable events—in this case, unexpectedly heavy snowstorms—upset the normal activities and expenditures of local authorities.[1] The environment was "lurking" below the surface—the opportunity it offered was not obvious. The company uncovered a situation—a Lurking Situation—that affected its own industry, and this was the genesis of a decision.

In 1984, more than 70 percent of the 65+ population owned their own

----

1. From a story reported in *The Wall Street Journal,* 4 Sept., 1984

homes. Some 84 percent of this number had paid off their mortgages in full. Two thirds of those over 65 had annual incomes of less than $14,000. Assume you are a mortgage broker. Are there any hidden opportunities for your company here? American Homestead, a New Jersey mortgage bank, was impressed by the 65+ population data and developed a mortgage plan that would pay a homeowner of 62 years or older a monthly amount, accruing as a loan secured by the house. The loan is repayable with interest when the homeowner moves or dies, and the house is sold. Prudential Bache Mortgage Company of America, joining American Homestead in the new project, services this market and charges significantly less than the conventional mortgage rates.[2] There was no obvious change in the environment, but American Homestead related the data describing the 65+ population to its own industry and found a new opportunity. It recognized a Lurking Situation and did something about it.

The marketing management at Kimberly Clark Corporation took a hard look at the estimated 100 million people in this country who annually suffer from serious colds. One of the reasons for this high figure is the spreading of germs from person to person. Kimberly Clark applied its know-how for making cleansing tissues to this Lurking Situation. The management decided to test market a new brand of Kleenex which was manufactured using medications that, the company claimed, would snuff out cold germs within seconds of using the tissue.[3] By understanding this environment, the company was able to discover a new market opportunity.

Nintendo is a household name to U.S. families with children. During the 1980s some 20 million Nintendo video games were sold, virtually saturating the market, with systems in about 90 percent of homes with children of game-playing age. This is a remarkable achievement, and many managements would be satisfied with this huge market share. But Nintendo saw in it a Lurking Situation in the making. The company saw an opportunity to translate at least a portion of the enthusiasm for video games into educational activities. To this end, in 1990 Nintendo donated $3 million to the Massachusetts Institute of Technology's Media Laboratory, in the hope that ''MIT can find ways to help create games that stimulate thought.''[4] In this way, the company sought to unlock the educa-

----

2. From a story reported in *The Wall Street Journal,* 4 Sept., 1984
3. From a story reported in *The Wall Street Journal,* 21 Aug., 1984
4. From a story reported in *The Wall Street Journal,* 15 May, 1990

tional market while capitalizing on the excitement caused by the games themselves.

Minor, seemingly unimportant incidents, can also call our attention to "lurking" situations. One such incident I remember concerned a little gray-haired lady who turned up at the annual shareholders' meeting of a major food processing firm. She cornered the chairman of the board during a coffee break and complained—in a pleasant way—about the packaging of a major brand of cereal. She found the box difficult to open. The chairman politely expressed his appreciation for her concern. And, he did something about it. He passed the complaint down to the brand's product manager who, in turn, was smart enough to pursue the lady's thought further. An informal survey among purchasers of the brand revealed a degree of dissatisfaction with the way the box opened—sufficient to justify considering a change. Here was a Lurking Situation uncovered by nothing more than the voicing of one person's thoughts.

· ·

Responding to New Environments

Among the uncounted decisional environments emerging daily in all industries, many are right in your own backyard—your company, your department. In some instances you may only need to be prompted to see an opening or a reason for change. In others you may need to search for the significance to your organization of changed or new environments. With today's proclivity for data and information, constant observation and incisive analyses should be uppermost in your mind, aimed at answering one question: "Is this new environment one that should cause us to consider some adjustment, some change, or something new and different?"

Understanding Data: Environmental vs. Actionable Data

Understanding and responding to the environment depends on how well you use the information or data available to your organization. Throughout this book, we will refer to data of two types: *environmental* and *actionable data*. Environmental data describe an environment or situation itself,

Source: © 1986. Reprinted with special permission of North America Syndicate.

whereas actionable data refer to the information used to take action in adjusting to that environment. We will deal with actionable data in a later chapter but, to distinguish the two types clearly, let's look at an example.

Environmental data are communicated to the decision makers *before* any possible courses of action are formulated. A salesperson who, after calling on customers, reports back that another company is introducing a competing product in the marketplace is providing environmental data. The information has come to light prior to formulating any possible courses of action. It is, therefore, purely environmental. Let's say the marketing manager conducts a survey to determine how well the competitor's new product is selling. The aim is to compile data for evaluating any impact on the company's sales and market share. Again, this information is still environmental because it is used before any counter-moves to react to the competitor's threat are posed. Now, suppose that marked inroads into the company's market are discovered, and the marketing manager decides that some response is necessary. The alternative courses of action subsequently developed could include such actions as a price reduction, increased advertising, or a change to the existing product. With these options in mind, the next issue is: Which of these choices should be selected?

And, on what basis should the decision be made? At this point, the management must seek additional data directed specifically at determining which of the options under consideration would be best for the company. These additional, more precise data refer directly to possible actions and are, therefore, *actionable* data.

Often, environmental and actionable data are obtained simultaneously during a single information-gathering effort. Some studies may seek specific actionable data, and the more general, environmental data are uncovered as a by-product. However, for purposes of discussion, let's treat them separately and find out how each affects the ways decisions are made. The remainder of this chapter will focus on environmental information and how it is used to uncover possible courses of action in the decision-making process.

Internal Environmental Data

Accounting Data

Internal environmental information is generated from within the organization. The key source in most companies is the organization's accounting records, from which a financial picture of past and present performance can be drawn. Potential future performance can also be predicted.

Accounting data are particularly valuable for the accurate, historical records that they can provide. They record the *past,* chronicling the performance of the company, its products, its sales territories, its production levels, and just about every other area of business operations. Marketing, in contrast, uses this information to build a picture of the potential *future* of the organization. Accountants produce financial statements which, over time, enable decision makers to recognize changes or new environments. Deviations from the Expected most often show up in accounting records, as inconsistencies emerge from year to year, from branch to branch, or from department to department.

A technique used to highlight the significance of financial data is the *ratio analysis.* In marketing, for example, comparison of ratios can enable you to monitor any deviations from expected sales levels or from expected sales costs. To illustrate, data for one quarter may reveal expense account totals of sales representatives as a percentage of that quarter's sales. Let's say expenses for one quarter are ten percent above a corresponding figure for the previous period. In the context of past operations, you judge this variance to be unusual, and decide it warrants further examination. A breakout of financial information by sales territory reveals that two districts have inordinately high expense account-to-sales ratios. A further analysis of the environment would be the basis for deciding which courses of action could be taken to correct the disparity.

The list of meaningful ratios you can work up from accounting records is endless, and they can be applied specifically to various types of business or various business functions. Some typical environmental ratios are as follows.

1. Expense-to-sales ratios

    (a) Advertising expense as percentage of sales

    (b) Selling expense as percentage of sales

    (c) Administrative expense as percentage of sales

    (d) Logistics expense as percentage of sales

2. Inventory situations

    (a) Turnover frequency

    (b) Order backlog as percentage of sales

    (c) Inventory to average dealer inventory

3. Results-to-marketing effort ratios

    (a) Average sales per call

    (b) Average sales per order

    (c) Sales to marketing effort

    (d) Profit to marketing investment

Keep in mind that ratio analysis uncovers information that is *environmental* in nature. It does not tell you what to do; it simply unearths situations that might require attention and, possibly, adjustment.

Informal Communications

Information flow within any organization can be improved through good internal communications. Internal communications—both informal and formal—can be an important source of information that affect business operations.

Peters and Waterman, in *In Search of Excellence,* stress the advantages of what they call "organizational fluidity." The thought is not new, they point out, but what "is new is that excellent companies seem to know how to make good use of it. Whether it's their rich ways of communicating informally or their special ways of using *ad hoc* devices, such as task forces, the excellent companies get quick action just because their organizations are fluid.

"The nature and use of communications in the excellent companies are remarkably different from those of their non-excellent peers. The excellent companies are vast networks of informal, open communications. The patterns cultivate the right people's getting into contact with each other, regularly. . . . What does it all add up to? Lots of communications. . . ."[5]

When R. Gordon McGovern assumed the presidency of Campbell Soup during the 1980s, he found the company unprepared for his informal approach to obtaining information. He would wander through the Campbell corridors every day and roam through supermarkets. He would constantly talk to people. McGovern's weekly new product sessions were attended by financial, marketing, engineering, and sales people who were subjected to such questions as, "Would you eat something like that?" Or, "Have you tried the competition's product?" He frequently showed "little reticence about short-circuiting the chain of command." One manager said, "McGovern put us on our toes." Another commented, "We are overloaded, but it's fun." McGovern believed that the open exchange of thoughts and ideas, despite position on the company hierarchy, can be an endless source of information.

Within your organization, your own personnel can hold the keys to new opportunities. Do not underestimate the power of good communications to uncover new information about the business or market environment, to which some adjustment may be worthwhile.

The Suggestion Box

The company suggestion box can be an excellent internal information source. Corny as it might seem, the suggestion box (a vast improvement over the "complaints box") can also lead to new opportunities. The advantages are obvious. An employee can make a suggestion, no matter

----
5. Thomas J. Peters and Robert H. Waterman, Jr., *In Search of Excellence,* New York, Harper & Row, 1982, p. 121

what its merit, without the risk of looking foolish in front of others. Especially when motivated by rewards for good ideas, the suggestion box has proven time and again to be the source of fertile, previously unrecognized information about the environment.

External Environmental Data

External environmental data consist of information amassed from sources outside your organization. They are usually non-accounting in nature and describe situations outside the company's own business operations. They may, for example, describe competitors, their market share, their pricing policies, and so on.

Surveys and Reports: Situation Audits

External data can be gathered through a variety of means, through research reports or surveys, through customer feedback, through reports and comments from sales representatives. Performance research on customers and prospects, production employees, retailers, sales staff, and the like can provide meaningful environmental data. Studies can range from those based on large national samples of people or firms, to small informal group discussions.

Let's look at some examples that show how external information gathered through simple surveys can be used to act as the springboard for possible action.

A survey of paper towel preferences among homemakers revealed a distinct trend in favor of Brand A as the age groups became older, as shown in Exhibit 3.1.

EXHIBIT 3.1   Paper towel preferences among homemakers, by age

	Homemakers by Age Bracket					
	18–25	*26–35*	*36–45*	*46–54*	*55+*	*Total*
Prefer Towel *A*	30%	32%	40%	51%	55%	39%
Prefer Towel *B*	70%	68%	60%	49%	45%	61%
Number of Interviews	395	485	640	345	190	2,005

Source: William F. O'Dell, Andrew C. Ruppel, Robert H. Trent, and William J. Kehoe, *Marketing Decision Making,* Fourth Edition, South-Western Publishing Co., Cincinnati, 1988, p. 37.

The company producing Brand *A* could use these data to make decisions on how best to adjust to this environment. The company might redirect its advertising message to the older age groups. It could repackage its product to appeal more strongly to them. Or it could alter its product to compete more directly with Brand *B*. Performance research, based on external environmental data, brought a Lurking Situation to light, thus initiating the decision process.

Another illustration. You work for a television manufacturer, and are in charge of its country-wide maintenance services. You authorize a study among persons who have owned a television for one year or more, restricting the survey to those owning the top three bestselling makes. One of the questions in the survey relates to the owners' ''degree of satisfaction'' with repair or maintenance services. You are with the company manufacturing Brand *A*. The external data in Exhibit 3.2 shows that for reasons not established by the data themselves, your customers are more dissatisfied with your product than those who own the two competing makes. Again, performance research uncovers a Lurking Situation, suggesting that the company respond to this environment. A follow-up study could, most likely, pinpoint the reasons for Brand *A*'s poor maintenance services.

EXHIBIT 3.2   Owner satisfaction with television maintenance services

Service required has been:	Brand A	Brand B	Brand C
Much less than expected	15%	36%	48%
Somewhat less than expected	16%	31%	33%
About as expected	10%	5%	3%
Somewhat more than expected	35%	20%	11%
Much more than expected	24%	8%	5%
Number of owners interviewed	322	277	301

This approach to collecting performance information is sometimes termed a *situation audit.* It is a survey of opportunities, threats, strengths, and weaknesses that might be exploited for the good of the company. Situation audits are used to analyze the trends and forces that have the greatest potential significance for the firm. A typical situation audit would consist of a series of survey questions that focus on an analysis of customers and markets, an evaluation of competition, an assessment of financial performance of the firm, or a summary of the political, technological, social or legal trends in the industry. A successful audit can highlight environments to which some adjustments should be made.

Information Services

How do you go about obtaining all this information? Well, unless you have the talent within your own four walls, and few firms do, you should think in terms of employing competent, professional help. A variety of skills are required, depending on the nature of the audit. Professional consultancies may specialize in finance, production, marketing, labor relations, personnel, purchasing, or other managerial areas. Financial management consultants are plentiful. Marketing consultants range from those specializing in *ad hoc* surveys, to those offering syndicated services, such as A. C. Nielson, best known for its media research and TV ratings services. Nielson also offers such services as consumer purchase information, providing data that not only reveal sales to customer ratios, but that also can be used to evaluate the effectiveness of promotional efforts.

No matter what your industry or company needs, there will be a syndicated service that can help. You can find data on, for example, want-ad volumes in newspapers, machine tool performances, or economic trends. There are financial data on ''household flow of funds,'' showing how national samples of households invest their money. You can find omnibus surveys on almost every subject, including monthly studies on the economic outlook of American families, and consumer data for different product categories and brands, and on buying patterns and consumer behavior.

Published Secondary Sources

External data are also available from secondary published sources. Often secondary source data are less specific, and have the reputation of being very dull reading. However, rapid advances in computer technology mean that information that once took weeks, months, or even years to amass and interpret, can now be accessed and analyzed meaningfully in minutes.

The number and variety of published secondary sources of environmental data are too great to describe. However, as an example let's look at one major source that is commonly used by industries, no matter what their specialization. This source is the published reports of the U.S. Census Bureau.

All taxpayers contribute to the gathering of secondary data for the

U.S. Census. It is a unique information source, organized and stored to allow flexible access, and available at low cost. As of 1990, the entire head count of the U.S. is available on computer disks, as well as on magnetic tape. This allows much easier and faster manipulation than was previously the case.

As well as uncovering general trends in population growth, or in the rate of household formulation, census data can be used for more specific purposes. One census file that provides extremely useful information is the *Tiger File*. It is an incredibly detailed geographical map of the U.S. that precisely locates every political subdivision, every street and road, every bridge and tunnel. All the information is expressed in digital form that can be stored and manipulated by computer. In 1990, the Census Bureau began merging the Tiger File with population information, placing people on the Tiger File maps. This makes the Tiger File a valuable tool of unlimited use for industry. Private research companies offer services that combine census data and consumer buying behavior data. In this way, as many as 240,000 census neighborhoods can be classified in terms of as few as 40 life-style categories.

Of course, secondary sources other than the census abound. Trade associations, business publishers, and university research bureaus can all contribute useful environmental data, some at no cost.

How such information is employed by decision makers varies greatly. However, as it is environmental in nature, it can be used to uncover existing or new situations to which the organization must adjust if it is to stay ahead.

So far, then, we have looked at the role of environmental information in initiating the decision-making process. It is gathered prior to the formation of and aids the development of alternative courses of action. This takes us to the next phase of the decision-making process: Once we have discovered a new or changed environment, we must formulate the possible courses of action we can take to best respond to it. This is the subject of the next chapter.

4

DEVELOPING ALTERNATIVE COURSES OF ACTION

Why do organizations need to react to changed or new environments? The answer is, of course, that organizations need to keep apace of change simply in order to survive and prosper in today's business world. How well you, your product or service, your organization, and your industry adapt to new situations will dictate your success or failure.

Forbes dramatizes this point by looking at the top ten U.S. companies

THE WALL STREET JOURNAL

"Saw my first robin today—just in time, too!"

Source: © 1985. From *The Wall Street Journal*. Permission, Cartoon Features Syndicate

of the 1970s and, 15 years later, showing how they fared.[1] The firms studied were Avon Products, Heublein, Eastman Kodak, Coca-Cola, Sperry & Hutchinson, Polaroid, Merck, American Home Products, Magnavox, and Xerox. Says *Forbes*, "What is striking to the observer looking back from a vantage point 15 years later is how few of them could make the adjustments necessary to stay on top."

Three of these companies, Heublein, Sperry & Hutchinson, and Magnavox, were bought out and no longer exist as independent organizations. None of the three is faring well in its new home. Xerox, says *Forbes*, "survived and grew. But its sharp drop in profitability put it near the bottom in its office equipment group for the past 12 months. . . . Polaroid managed to maintain its market share in instant photography, but at the cost of a return on equity so low—under five percent—that it could have been improved by buying bank certificates of deposit. . . . Even formidable Eastman Kodak, Polaroid's big competitor that once dominated the market, is not without its problems. . . . It is hard to believe that, a scant decade ago, Avon Products was one of the shining glories of the economy

———————

1. *Forbes*, 14 Jan., 1985, p. 41

and the stock market. . . . Avon's latest 12-month return on equity was a full ten percentage points below its five year average . . . falling afoul of the most powerful of tides, cultural change.''

Adjusting to change is an issue as important to the smallest start-up company as it is to these industrial giants. And the reasons why businesses fail to respond well to change are the same. Eric Hofer argues that Americans don't really like change (and he's certainly right on that!).[2] Even in unimportant things, change can be traumatic. Common reasons for our resistance to change in business operations, declares Hofer, are:

- It's against policy

- We've never done it that way

- It won't work

- No one will accept it

- It's too radical

These five reasons may oversimplify the issue, but all of us can identify with one or more of them. I would add one more: fear of failure. This explains why, for example, manufacturers tend to play it safe by bringing out modifications of existing product lines far more often than they launch completely new, innovative products.

••

The Need to Develop Alternative Courses of Action

The scene is southwest Florida. Long-time tennis star Jimmy Connors and associated investors have built a $100 million international tennis center, health spa, and resort just four miles south of a residential area. The complex includes two condominium buildings and a world-class hotel, plus a tennis arena seating some 5000 spectators. Additional facilities are planned. Four miles in the other direction, a lush riverfront community is opening, with a

----
2. Brightman, Harvey J., *Problem Solving: A Logical and Creative Approach,* Georgia State University, Atlanta, 1980, p. 25

championship golf course, and almost twice as many tennis courts as the Connors' site. Other developments proposed include a 200-room resort hotel, with a 250-slip marina to complete the picture. The new community, when fully occupied, will house some 7500 persons.

How do nearby residents of the area react to these changes? Overall, reactions are negative. True, the developments will enhance the prestige of the community, but they will bring more people to the roads, crowd the restaurants, and life will be just a bit more hustled.

This is an example of a newly-developed situation (the Threat) over which people have no control but to which they must adapt. Before taking any action to respond to the situation, the residents must first find out what their options are. In this case, they may endure the encroachments—which, after all, are bearable and bring compensations—or they may decide to move to less crowded areas.

The example serves to illustrate what happens in the second phase of the decision-making process outlined at the beginning of the book. As we saw in the previous chapter, in Phase 1 we recognize that a changed environment exists and we find out as much as we can about it. In Phase 2 we list the options we can take to react to that environment.

. . . .
Constraints to Developing Options

As we have seen, business decisions are rarely made alone. No individual and no department operates—nor should they operate—in a vacuum. Your colleagues, other departments, top management, your shareholders, and others within your industry will all affect the ways in which options are identified. Moreover, they may all be impacted by the alternatives you select. It is important, therefore, to understand the constraints within which options can reasonably be developed.

The first issue to consider is company policy, which can dictate which courses of action are possible and which are off-limits. Imagine you are the personnel manager of a manufacturing corporation. Your productivity is suffering because of an acute shortage of certain types of workers. One option open to you is to lower the criteria presently used in hiring, and therefore attract more, less-skilled applicants. A second option is to maintain the same demanding criteria but to solicit actively applications from experienced em-

"Earnings are down again. Should we reorganize or find scapegoats?"

ployees at a rival organization by offering wages above the current market level. This latter alternative may provide a quicker solution to the problem, but it violates company policy and is therefore not viable. Your options are limited to those that support the overall policies of the organization.

Developing options, because it affects policy in this way, is part of the strategic decision-making process of the organization. All the options you choose must conform to overall corporate strategy, and within that to product strategy, financial strategy, production strategy, advertising strategy, or any other level of strategy within the organization. If they do not, they are either not reasonable courses of action, or they indicate that a change in strategy—creating a new business environment—is required.

Before we go any further, let's make certain we agree on the meaning of strategy and we know how strategy differs from tactics. Strategy planning locates and defines the road down which the organization plans to travel to reach its objective. No funds are allocated to the development of strategy. It is the guiding force that gives direction to the company's activities, all the while recognizing corporate objectives and the resources available.

Whatever the industry or business, and whatever the environmental situation, strategy directs decision making. Let's say the corporate goal for a particular branded product is an increase in market share from 15 to 20 percent. The advertising strategy is to contribute to this overall objective by boosting sales to non-users of the product. This means that the advertiser's *tactics*—the choice of media and copy themes—should be aimed not at attracting customers of competing brands, but at persuading non-users to buy. The alternatives chosen must conform to that stated strategy.

How, then, do tactics differ from strategy? Tactics are, simply, the means through which strategies are carried out. In advertising, as we have seen, tactics might include decisions on the media selected, how much we invest, and the style of copy or visuals we use. These are all tactical advertising decisions that are directed by a broader strategy. Production tactics might be decisions on new product designs, package revisions, or other operational changes. Unlike strategic decisions, tactical decisions require specific investment. In brief, strategy allocates resources; tactics expend them. Both place constraints on optional courses of action.

Another factor which may constrain the development of certain options is their efficiency in achieving stated goals. Most firms—with the possible exception of not-for-profit organizations—primarily seek survival, growth, and profit. Their long-term objectives and strategy are directed at staying in business and rewarding owners, employees, customers, and communities. It follows, then, that all decision alternatives must have the same aims. They must be developed with the purpose of maximizing profit and growth.

We can look at the efficiency of possible decision alternatives in terms of the degree to which they optimize the opportunity for growth. *Full optimization* is beyond the reach of most organizations. It requires that all alternatives to which the firm's resources could be allocated be assessed in terms of the contribution they make toward maximizing growth and profit. To do this, decision makers must know all the possible impacts of each alternative on the entire organization. For full optimization we need to have control over everything that could possibly impact the organization, including outside events. This means that every possible decision must maximize to the utmost the growth and profitability of the firm.

Obviously, in a business world fraught with change and overloaded with information, this is not possible and only *partial optimization* can realistically be expected. But partial optimization, too, boggles the mind and is difficult to achieve. For example, if you pose options that will reduce costs of a particular operation, the chances are that each change will inadvertently affect other areas of the organization, and can increase costs or reduce revenue elsewhere. Suppose you consider the option of lowering your advertising expenditure. This might save money in the short term, but you risk reducing sales, thus increasing the per-unit manufacturing cost of the product. The difficulty is that you cannot measure or compare precisely the effects of alternative courses of action. There are too many variables.

Sub-optimization results when alternatives are selected without considering the possible impacts on the different profit centers within the organization. Thus, the profitability of one department might increase, but at the cost of reducing the profitability of others. One reason that companies operate at sub-optimal levels is that the different departments find it difficult to compare objectively the alternatives facing them in terms appropriate for the entire firm.

By understanding the principles of optimization, we can see clearly why decisions must be made with the whole organization, its corporate strategy, and its objectives in view. Each decision made and each allocation of funds can cause a ripple effect throughout the organization, impacting on the productivity levels of different departments: inefficiency and ineffectiveness result.

Alternatives must be selected to the extent feasible and appropriate, not on their individual or short-term merits, but on the basis of how well they can contribute to overall profitability. With this in mind, let's move on to look at how alternatives are born and developed.

Creating Options

When most of us think of creativity, we think of artistic people, such as musicians, painters, novelists, or performers. But creativity is possible in

DUNAGIN'S PEOPLE

"OUR QUALITY CONTROL IS OUT OF CONTROL AND PRODUCT FAILURE IS AT AN ALL-TIME HIGH. CLEARLY, THE THING TO DO IS INCREASE OUR ADVERTISING BUDGET."

Source: © 1986. Reprinted with special permission of North America Syndicate

all walks of life, and business is no exception. Think of the Research and Development department of your organization, and how it contributes to decision making. Compared to some of us, the R&D people may seem to have soft jobs: we have an image of them sitting around, dreaming, and gazing at the blue sky. They always seem to have adequate funds. They are scientific, yet creative. They ignore deadlines. They have the ear of top management. Fact is, though, management charges R&D with one heavy responsibility: the formation of alternatives. R&D does not make the final decisions, but there is a constant pressure to come up with new ideas: to be creative.

Creativity is important, however, to *all* decision makers. How creative and how perceptive you are in identifying alternative courses of action reflects your willingness and ability to adjust to changing environments. Creativity is the single most important ingredient of successful business decision making in a competitive environment—bar none. The reason is simple: The creative person develops decision alternatives that do not occur to the non-creative. And it is ideas that are unique to your organization that will give you an edge over the competition.

Linked to creativity is innovation. Creativity is thinking up new things. Innovation is putting them into action in new and unique ways. Harvard's Ted Levitt claims, "There is no shortage of creativity or creative people in American business. The shortage is of innovators." He argues that "all too often, people believe that creativity leads to innovation. It doesn't."[3]

Applying these observations to business decision making, then, creativity centers on the decision maker's ability to recognize a situation requiring change. Innovation is the ability to respond by devising unique, relevant, and practicable ways to adjusting to that need for change.

In some instances, the need for change is imposed—it is a reaction to the Threat as when, for example, a competitor changes the market price of a product. In others, it is voluntary, as when an opportunity for change is discovered from observing a Lurking Situation in the business environment, and alternatives are developed to take advantage of that unique situation. The options that emerge represent innovation—the application of new ideas to cope effectively with change.

Suppose a competitor creates a new, threatening environment by lowering the price on a brand product in your line. How you react depends on your creativity as a business organization. Sure, you can act predictably and meet the new price level. All you will achieve, however, is a reduction in your profit margin and that of your competitor. You need a more creative, less obvious response. What might you consider? You could change your product formula. You could increase your advertising effort, or change the focus of your advertising. You could alter your distribution system. You could work out new incentive plans for your dealers or your sales staff. You could *increase* the price of your brand, and thereby achieve a new market positioning. Even a Threat, therefore, can be transformed into unlimited opportunities for creativity and for innovation.

Encouraging Creativity

True creativity in the business field is rare. Both as a business professional and while running courses in decision making, I have held brainstorming

----
3. Levitt, Theodore, "Ideas Are Useless Unless Used," in *inc.*, Feb. 1981, p. 96

sessions to encourage creativity. No matter how well-experienced or how highly-educated the participants in a group, it always surprises me that most of the creative ideas that are suggested—including the very best ones—come from the same one or two individuals in the group. While most business people are good at basing their ideas on logic, precision, and quantitative data, few take a truly creative approach.

Can a person increase his or her creativity, or the creativity of others within an organization? The answer must be a resounding "yes." Most people must overcome the obstacles of years of education where creativity is stifled. From early elementary school through college, educators stress precision, logic, accuracy, neatness, and detail. Analysis is extolled as opposed to free wheeling original thought. You can encourage creativity by placing people in situations that stimulate imagination, speculation, the exchange of ideas, thought association, and observation.

The brainstorming session is a common technique that businesses use to encourage and benefit from new ideas. Imagine a group meeting, the goal of which is to generate ideas for new product lines. Before they get together, the participants saturate themselves with information about the broad product category in which they plan to expand. The brainstorming session is the forum at which they voice a wide range of ideas, from the most logical and well-thought out to the most impulsive and instinctive, from the sublime to the ridiculous. The sole purpose of the meeting is to solicit as broad a selection of ideas as possible. No ideas, no matter how ineffectual or how bizarre they may seem, are judged, evaluated, criticized, or rejected. All are heard and listed for later analysis outside the meeting.

Brainstorming is an excellent tool for encouraging new and different perspectives. It becomes practicable once the wide range of alternatives is narrowed from the uninhibited list to the more feasible options. This is sometimes accomplished through *reverse brainstorming,* during which the group discusses all the limitations, problems, and weaknesses of each concept and eliminates all but those most likely to succeed.

Maximizing your powers of observation is another means of cultivating creativity. Watch your customers, listen to the questions they ask and the complaints and suggestions they raise. These can be a valuable source of inspiration. The value leading industries place on customer response is reflected in the increasing popularity of toll-free 800 numbers, which invite customers to call and voice their opinions. Procter & Gamble claims that within a year it got 200,000 calls on its 800 number, ". . . calls with customer ideas or complaints. . . . Insiders report that the 800 number is a major source of product improvement ideas.'"[4]

Let's look at some examples in which observation of the business and market environments has led to highly creative opportunities.

The innovative product line of undershorts for men, developed by Jockey International, Inc., resulted from an observation by one of the company's top executives. Noticing that women on a Florida beach wore bikinis not only for swimming but as casual beachwear, he mused: "Why don't we make a similar product for men?" Thus, out of this simple observation came the highly profitable Jockey undershorts line.

In 1952 Bill Bowerman[5] was a track coach at the University of Oregon. He knew about sore feet. He watched his athletes run with sore feet, caused by the inadequacy of the track shoes then available. He saw tennis players and basketball players with similar problems. Looking further afield, he noticed that non-athletes, too, wanted to run, play tennis, or just walk without suffering from sore feet.

In those days, virtually the same shoe went on every athlete, despite the differing demands of various sports. Bowerman thought each sport could justify its own shoe, shaped for particular movements and stress points. He offered improved designs for different sports to several U.S. sports equipment manufacturers but none was accepted. They each turned down the opportunity to innovate.

So Bowerman became a shoemaker. He worked with area cobblers and bootmakers, developing sketches of athletes' shoes that were sleek and light, and that were designed around the needs of particular sports. He outfitted his own track team with custom-built shoes. He experimented, and changed the shoes through time.

That was the beginning of Blue Ribbon Sports, later to become Nike, named after the Greek goddess of victory. Today Nike is a multi-million dollar operation, competing with established shoe firms as well as numerous newcomers. And it all began when Bill Bowerman perceived a business opportunity—or a Lurking Situation—that led to required creativity and innovation.

----

4. Peters and Waterman, *op. cit.,* p. 194
5. Discussion on Bowerman drawn from P. Ranganeth Nayak and John M. Ketteringham, *Breakthroughs,* Arthur D. Little, Inc., Boston, 1986

. . . .

Mini-Decisions

Before we examine in detail how alternative courses of action are collected, let's make sure we agree on what constitutes a decision option.

A decision is that part of the decision-making process that results in
a given course of action. You fire a foreman, you agree to a bank loan,
you lower your price, you allocate $100,000 to a merchandising pro-
motion. Each of these actions resulted from selecting one of at least two
alternatives. Either you fire the foreman or you don't. You drop your
brand's retail price from $4.19 to $3.99, or you maintain the original
price. You allocate $100,00, rather than $200,000. The final decision
in each instance is, of course, one of the alternatives listed. A decision,
then, is the selection of one of two or more actionable options under
consideration.

Let's assume several different options have been posed. One suggestion is that before any alternative is selected over the others, more information be gathered so that a better-informed, actionable decision can be
taken. This option, to obtain additional data, constitutes a new decision in
itself. It is *not,* however, a main, actionable decision alternative. Instead,
it is a move to aid in the making of an actionable decision. It is what we will
call a *mini-decision.*

Let's say you belong to a committee within the trust department of a
bank. The following alternatives are open to you.

1. Purchase U.S.A. Treasury Note Series B, 1996

2. Do not purchase the Note

3. Obtain more data before deciding between #1 or #2.

Options #1 and #2 are actionable alternatives; #3 is not. It is not part of the
decision-making process that will directly result in a course of action. Instead, it is a "wheel-within-a-wheel" that requires its own new decision-
making process. This might involve, for example, selecting the method
for securing additional information, and determining how much time and
money to spend on the project. Thus, delaying a decision in favor of obtaining more data is not an option in the broader, actionable decision
making sense. Many a committee flounders on this point. In developing
alternatives, therefore, make sure that you and your committee under-

stand the difference between an actionable and a mini-decision, and focus your discussions accordingly.

. . . .
Putting Together a List of Alternatives

A key rule to follow in all aspects of consensus decision making is to put everything down in writing for all to see. This is particularly important when developing a list of alternative courses of action. No matter how this list is created—through meetings, through brainstorming, or through individual suggestions—make sure that you write down every possible option and that everyone involved has a chance to see the list as it grows. The advantage is twofold: first, writing down alternatives eliminates or reduces any misunderstanding or disagreement on what has been voiced; second, it tests your ability to present options in clear, unambiguous language. An additional benefit is that you produce a record of all that has been stated and can later trace actions back to the ideas stage. This might help in future decision making.

It is important that while the list is being put together, no judgments or criticisms are made of the options included. Too early a discussion of the relative merits of the decision options could preclude the listing of the very one that might be chosen after full and complete deliberation. List as many options as you can think of. As in brainstorming, encourage any and all possible ideas. Though in some cases you will find that ''go'' and ''no go'' are the only viable courses of action for you, try not to stop at just these two alternatives. Lee Iacocca makes this point. He tells that he never likes to settle for ''either chocolate or vanilla.'' He always wants to include ''strawberry'' as one of the options. It makes sense. Once you think your list is complete with three, four or five options, add a sixth or seventh alternative. This will allow more scope for discussion—and for creativity.

Let's assume, for example, you are considering increasing the price of your product. Your initial choices could look like this:

1. Increase price of product

2. Keep price at $4.19

Source: DENNIS THE MENACE® Used by permission of Hank Ketcham and © by North America Syndicate

These two options are self-limiting. An improved set of options would be:

1. Increase price of product to $4.59

2. Increase price of product to $4.39

3. Keep price at $4.19

This allows more room for discussion and is more likely to make the decision makers think of the specific effects of each price raise. It is also more likely to generate creative ideas on how each option might be put into action.

Organizing the List

Let's say you are the vice-president of marketing with a consumer goods company. You call an advertising meeting, the purpose of which is to allocate an advertising budget of $5 million among various media. The budgeted figure has previously been approved by your financial people. Your advertising agency has furnished these data on the past year's allocations:

1. Spot TV $3,000,000

2. Weekly news magazines $1,000,000

3. Newspapers $1,000,000

As the conference warms up into a free-flowing session, the list of options grows. The committee tosses a variety of thoughts upon the table, resulting in the following alternatives:

1. Increase the advertising appropriation by $2 million

2. Double the number of newspapers being used, cutting the amount of space used in each

3. Increase the budget allocation for weekly news magazines to $2 million

4. Increase spot TV to $4,000,000, dropping national magazines and newspapers to half last year's figures

5. Continue the present allocation among the three media

6. Change the basic advertising theme to one stressing flavor and taste in place of health

The options are diverse and each demands that different factors be considered and that different departments be consulted. Before any progress can be made, the alternatives need to be organized.

There are three steps in organizing options, and we will look at each in turn.

1. Separate the alternatives into distinct decision structures

2. Make certain the alternatives are mutually exclusive (i.e. they do not overlap)

3. Sequence the decision structures

Look again at the initial list of six alternatives above. How many decision structures can you identify in the list? There are four. Look at alternative #1. This is the only option that will affect the whole advertising appropriation. The issue implied by alternative #1 is whether to increase or decrease the budget, or whether to keep it at last year's level. The other five options neither conflict with or depend upon this course of action. It has its own decision structure. Alternative #2 also has its own decision structure. None of the other options refers to the way in which newspaper space is used. (Note that alternative #4 refers to newspapers, but its focus is budget allocation rather than use of space.) The next three options, alternatives #3, #4, and #5, belong within the same decision structure because all three are related to the same issue to be resolved: allocating the media budget. They can be displayed on the same table, as below.

	Media allocations, in $ millions		
	#3	#4	#5
Weekly magazines	$2.0	$0.5	$1.0
Spot TV	?	4.0	3.0
Newspapers	?	0.5	1.0
Total	**$5.0**	**$5.0**	**$5.0**

Alternative #6 calls for a fourth decision structure, as it is the only option that refers to the advertising theme. The issue it implies is whether the ad theme should be changed, or whether it should remain the same.

We have thus reduced our list of six options, to a list of four decision structures. The list has been so organized that those alternatives that require similar considerations are grouped together.

Next, look at the four decision structures that remain. Are they independent of each other and mutually exclusive in terms of the action they require? Simple logic tells us that unless the alternatives are mutually exclusive, it is not possible to make a single choice from the options listed. Mutual exclusivity is essential so that when the alternatives are evaluated, each one is distinct. Options that overlap confuse the decision-making process.

A simple example. A toy manufacturer is considering revamping a mostly steel-made product, as a means of reducing the unit cost. The design group poses these options:

1. Make the toy shell of aluminum

2. Make the toy shell of plastic

3. Eliminate the existing motor from the newly-designed toy

Of course, these options are not mutually exclusive. The company could manufacture and market the product in either aluminum or plastic, and eliminate the motor at the same time. Make sure your options are properly worded and independent of each other so that one of them—and only one—can finally be chosen. In this example, option #3 might be better worded: manufacture the shell of the toy in steel, but eliminate the motor.

Another example. You are a finance officer at your company. You meet with production and marketing staff to agree on a strategy to combat competitive price maneuvering on a food product line. These alternatives emerge:

1. Reduce price to 49¢

2. Double advertising effort

3. Reduce product weight to 17 oz

Here, there are three possible decision structures and each requires a different course of action. The above three options are *not* mutually exclusive. The decision makers could agree to carry out all the alternatives listed.

Refining the initial list of alternatives, then, calls for placing the options into appropriate decision structures and making sure that the alternative courses of action do not overlap and are, therefore, mutually exclusive. The last step is to sequence the different decision structures. By sequencing, we mean resolving the order in which the decision alternatives will be considered. This can be done by prioritizing the decision structures in terms of the impact they may have on the organization. In terms of profit, the consequences of a wrong decision are greater when the decision involves, for example, doubling the advertising budget, than when it involves choosing either color or black and white printing. The strategic decision structure that pertains to the size of the budget should, of course, be considered before the *tactical* decision structure relating to use of color.

Another means of sequencing is to isolate those options that naturally depend on prior decisions being made. For example, a decision on whether to advertise in magazines would need to be resolved before alternatives are posed regarding page layouts. What to name a product usually waits until there is agreement on whether the new product should be introduced.

In general, strategic issues are to be considered prior to tactical issues. When sequencing the list of alternatives, keep asking yourself, ''Are we attacking the basic issue first?''

Agreeing on a Final List

At this stage, you should be home free, at least as far as formulating meaningful alternatives is concerned. If you have employed your creativity to the utmost, reduced the possible options to writing, refined the list by sorting the different choices into distinct decision structures, checked on mutual exclusivity, and sequenced the options so that you tackle the most basic issue first, you can move forward.

Unfortunately you must deal with people: the committee of which you are a part and which you may be chairing. Some member of the group is sure to slow you down by arguing about the phrasing or inclusion of one option or another. Whatever you do, don't proceed down the path of the DMP until you win him or her over to your side—or until you acquiesce. Change the phrasing, drop an option, do whatever is necessary to come to terms.

Unless you and your compatriots at this point have complete agreement on the alternatives and their precise phrasing you will rue the day when, later in the DMP, you find some group member insisting that you are recommending a course of action that was not even one of the options being considered. If you had agreement on the options, you win this one. But if you moved too fast, without the assent of all decision makers, you will find yourself on the horns of a dilemma—an embarrassing spot, especially when your boss is in the room.

But you are well above all that. So, let's move on to how the sophisticated decision maker goes about selecting one alternative over the others.

5

THE
CORE
CRITERION

A studied Marxist would not benefit from this book. It is for those who believe in competition, free enterprise, the essentiality of profit in our society, and survival of the fittest. This book aids the decision maker who recognizes opportunities and acts on them. The free enterprise system depends on individual initiative—millions of people who daily make decisions on behalf of their organizations in a free world.

There are "two obvious advantages of the free enterprise system.

First, on the average, over a moderate number of years, it yields the highest total output, and second, on the average, it adapts the pattern of production most closely to consumer wants. These advantages are directly visible to anyone who travels around the world. Contrast, for example, Western and Eastern Europe, Taiwan and the People's Republic of China."[1]

Capitalism offers "the promise of a bright future already on the horizon—when *average* life expectancy may approach 90 years, when products derived from recombinant DNA research will eliminate most viral diseases, when we will enjoy greater leisure, and (when) materials . . . will be stronger, and safer."[2]

The entire free enterprise system bases its success on the role profit plays in its daily activities. Each and every decision aims at enhancing profitability.

But don't confuse profit and greed. To maximize profit and disregard consumer wants leads to conditions that ultimately bring about the decline of the organization. Charging "what the traffic will bear" is an unsavory practice that places inordinately high profits on goods. However, the high prices charged for a product by a pharmaceutical manufacturer, for example, aimed at recovering its R&D expenditures spent in developing a new drug can well be justified—at least until the investment is recovered, and perhaps even longer in order to recoup some losses on earlier failures. In sharp contrast are the pricing policies of, for example, certain segments of the entertainment and publishing fields that knowingly embrace greed when they produce and promote questionable material to the adolescent market. Each spring college students converge on Florida. Brewers are out in force, encouraging young people to drink. One beer company in 1989 filled the lobby of a Daytona Beach hotel, selling beer by the case. So the kids got drunk, and some got killed falling off balconies. All in the name of profit? No: greed.

A land developer, failing to comprehend its responsibilities to community and country, made news when it earmarked a 542-acre tract adjacent to the Manassas National Battlefield Park in Virginia for an enormous

---

1. "The Advantage of the Free Enterprise System": *The American Free Enterprise System: Its Foundation and Prospects,* Neil H. Snyder, ed. McIntire School of Commerce, University of Virginia, 1984, p. 69

2. Mobil Corporation's "Lies they tell our children" advertisement, 1984

shopping mall. The developer's plan was to cover the ground of the epic struggle that ended with Robert E. Lee at the gates of Washington and the fragile Union at the brink of permanent dissolution. Preservationists were furious, and some months later the U.S. Congress was persuaded to purchase the land, precluding the developer's plan to commercialize the area. The developer placed profit above being a good citizen: greed.

Still, the line between profit and greed is sometimes a thin one, the difference being merely the subjective definition of the two terms. Those who abhor greed say that profits should be restricted in some undefined way by, it would appear, some "invisible hand." But the marketplace is an excellent control mechanism and can be effective in holding greed to a minimum.

Maximum, long-range, *socially acceptable* profit, then, motivates the decision maker. It is the basic, essential decision criterion—pervasive and persistent. "It lies at the very core of corporate goals and objectives, despite occasional euphemistic re-expressions of corporate aims. Ideally, therefore, every . . . alternative should be evaluated as to its production of profit."[3] More specifically, maximization of long-run profit—*socially acceptable profit*.

• •

What Is Profit?

Selection of criteria through which all the decision alternatives you have developed can be evaluated depends primarily on the long-term objectives of the organization. As we have seen, most business organizations seek survival and growth through maximizing profit. Profit, then, is their key corporate objective.

Profit is, in its simplest form, what is left over from revenue after costs have been deducted. By costs, we mean all expenditures needed to start up and keep a company running, including materials, equipment and labor costs, and costs of financing, inflation, taxes, and depreciation. In a profitable organization, there is a wide margin between revenue and costs: the profit margin. Though there are, of course, other,

---

3. *Op. cit.*, Stein, *The American Free Enterprise System*, p. 85

more sophisticated measures to determine how successful a business organization is, most of these—as we shall see—fall within the broad scope of maximizing profit.

There are, however, organizations whose objectives cannot be as narrowly defined as this. These are not-for-profit organizations that can have a variety of key objectives. Hospitals, trade associations, political groups, workers' unions, and charities, for example, each use different measures of performance. The criteria they use, therefore, in making decisions will not necessarily be profit-based. In a hospital, the goal—and, therefore, the criteria used to evaluate decision alternatives—might relate to the maximization of patient health. For a trade association, it might be to enhance the public image of an industry. For a political party, a goal might be to increase the likelihood of the electorate voting for issues supported by the group, and for a union, it might be to increase the number of members. Although in this chapter we will concentrate on increasing profit as a key corporate objective—and therefore as an issue central to establishing criteria for selecting decision alternatives—in the context of not-for-profit organizations, the focus should be shifted to the relevant goals that have been set.

Long-Range vs. Short-Range Profit

Every decision involves a prediction. When opting for a given choice over others, the decision maker predicts that the alternative selected will enhance long-range profits more than any other option under consideration. But long-range means several years down the road. Happenings six years or four years or even two years into an uncertain future defy accurate forecasting. Actions by others well beyond your company's control can play havoc with forecasts. The future is unknown; competitors, governments, and customers join in clouding your vision. The domestic economy and world political situation seem to mount campaigns aimed at reducing your long-range predicting to little more than a guess.

So what do you do? You draw on a less reliable criterion. Your best bet at this stage is *short-run* profitability. It can deceive, and in time a decision based on short-run profits can turn out to be wrong—as measured by the old standby of *long-range* profitability. It could be, though, that short-run profits represent the best available criterion when long-range profits simply cannot be predicted.

Consumer goods giant Procter & Gamble sometimes relies heavily on short-run profits as a predictor of long-range profitability, evidenced by the firm's frequent use of test marketing for many of its new products. The rationale is that if a relatively short period of testing reveals favorable data, then for the long-run the product is a good risk. In other words, when an adequate correlation is thought to exist between short- and long-run profits, management is encouraged to accept short-run results as predictive of the long-run. P&G's introduction of Liquid Tide emerged on the market after only two months of test marketing in Minneapolis.

But remember that the short-run criterion can lead you astray. Take another Procter & Gamble product after its introduction. "P&G's Duncan Hines cookies have . . . fallen short of expectations. Some analysts (say) the cookies, which are crisp on the outside and chewy on the inside, are not different enough from existing packaged cookies to glean the dramatic marketplace response that P&G anticipated. P&G officials say the cookies got off to a fast start, but were slowed by a rash of me-too entries from Nabisco, Keebler, and Frito-Lay."[4] So, if the Duncan Hines cookie sales were disappointing, it was due to the difficulty of being reasonably certain of a correlation between the short-run and the long-run. Competitors "contaminated" the long-range projections with their aggressive entries.

In summary, using short-run profitability as a predictive measure of whether to go in one direction rather than another may fall short of perfection, but it is vastly better than not having any measure at all.

· ·

Sales As a Decision Criterion

To foretell revenue, long-run and short-run, you must predict *sales* accurately. If you are in the process of deciding whether to introduce a new

------

4. Steven Greenhouse, "Slumbering giant Procter & Gamble wakes up to competition," *New York Times News Service,* 3 Mar. 1985

product, for example, forecasting the item's sales over the short-run or long-run is your assignment.

Hand in hand with sales projections goes an analysis of costs. As we have seen, the profit margin is calculated through measuring total revenue against total investment and operational costs. To get a true picture of a new product's feasibility, therefore, the sales forecast must be compared to the anticipated costs level.

Accurate and meaningful cost estimates depend to some extent on communication and cooperation within all departments of the organization. The financial people must forecast and arrange for the acquisition of adequate capital. Operations management must prepare production budgets and schedule its existing facilities and operations. Marketing management must plan such activities as pricing, packaging, distribution, and advertising. Only once all this information is brought together will you be able to predict the level of sales necessary to produce your new product at a profit. The level of profit you aim for will, of course, depend on your predictions with regard to market factors.

....

Surrogate Evaluation Criteria

There are many situations—perhaps most situations—where even the criterion of short-range profits cannot or should not be employed. This brings the decision makers to the brink, where they stand or fall.

In essence, it can be said that profit as the core criterion is dependent on predicting sales. But, we know that a precise prediction of sales is not always feasible. So, we look for another criterion—a surrogate criterion. Any substitute criterion is bound to be less reliable than sales (which can be related directly to profit), but the surrogate often is forced into the picture simply because predicting sales cannot be achieved with an acceptable degree of accuracy. It is essential that the surrogate criterion selected be highly correlated to long-range profitability.

One example of a surrogate criterion is *market share,* sometimes termed market penetration or market position. Market share represents your firm's percentage of the total industry, and its value as a criterion is dependent on your having a good picture of the industry's total sales. On occasions when sales cannot be predicted with precision, market share can

THE WALL STREET JOURNAL

"Estimated quarterly tax, $483.50...."

Source: © 1985, *The Wall Street Journal.* Reprinted by permission
of Cartoon Features Syndicate

be determined by conducting a survey to measure what share of the industry sales your product or service can garner. Then, knowing the value or
size of the total market, you compute the dollar sales and profitability—on
the short-run at least.

As mentioned earlier the nature of some products or services precludes
the employment of a criterion that involves obtaining test-market sales and
revenue data in advance of making the decision. When Ford was first considering the marketing of its Thunderbird, it was not feasible, of course, to
build hundreds of cars and test market the new make. Instead the Ford
management had to make the Go/No Go decision by using a surrogate criterion well short of the core criterion of maximizing long-run profits. The
marketing decision makers had to locate a criterion thought to be closely
related to sales and market share—a surrogate criterion. It was *consumer attitude* or *stated consumer intention to buy.* This criterion—obtained through the
use of prototypes far in advance of production—was employed in predicting
the future of the Thunderbird and, as subsequent sales have long since established, the criterion was a reliable one, even though it is far removed
from the core criterion of maximizing long-run profits.

It's another ball game when decisions are made by operations or production managements. Here, the criterion centers around lowest possible costs in keeping with acceptable performance. An electronics firm, let's say, has three production plants in the Midwest. Long-range strategy calls for adding to the firm's two present suppliers, both located within 150 miles of all three manufacturing facilities. The tactical issue is: Which of several acceptable suppliers should be added? The management employed the criterion of *transportation costs,* a surrogate for maximizing long-range profits.

The list of surrogate criteria goes on without end. Let's say you are an advertising manager and the alternative copy themes have been narrowed to two. You, quite obviously, wish to select the one that will contribute most to the company's long-run profits. But to engage in extensive research to determine which of the two themes would have the greater impact on increasing the firm's long-range profitability would be an economic waste. Better to select a substitute criterion that can be confidently assumed to correlate with greater sales. *Consumer awareness,* for example, would be appropriate. Or, *consumer recall* of the brand name.

It is probably safe to say that most of the business decisions made today are based on surrogate criteria, but in recognizing this remember the core criterion. If for some reason you can't measure and predict the impact of the various decision alternatives on long-range profitability, choose a surrogate criterion that in your judgment correlates (closely, you hope!) with the core criterion.

• •

Selecting the Most Appropriate Criteria

We have looked briefly at the types of criteria that can be used to evaluate different decision alternatives. The next step is to select those criteria that are most appropriate to the decision to be made.

This task becomes simpler if we look at the options under consideration and decide first whether they are *identical-cost* or *diverse-cost* alternatives.

Identical-cost alternatives are those which will result in the same level of expenditure. In other words, it would cost the same to put Option *A* into operation as it would to put Option *B* into operation. A choice be-tween two advertising themes, for example, for a 30-second radio spot, would involve the same level of cost. In such instances the decision makers must determine which one alternative to select, based on which is better *in terms of some criterion other than profitability*.

Remember, *how much* better is not a consideration. In the advertising theme illustration, the decision makers are down to two choices: A or B. Their job is to select one of the two. It doesn't matter how much better A is than B. So, when you are making identical-cost decisions, think in terms of surrogate criteria. Don't concern yourself about nailing down how much better one option is over the others in terms of dollars.

Diverse cost alternatives will result in different levels of cost. If the ad-vertising decision to be made was the choice between a 30-second radio spot and a 30-second television spot, the resultant costs would differ widely. Similarly, when an operations manager is deciding whether to purchase Stamping Machine *A* at $40,000, or Stamping Machine *B* at $60,000, this is a diverse-cost decision. Of course, multi-criteria, such as performance, durability, credit terms, delivery time, and reliability can also be used, but the bottom line will be to decide which option will con-tribute best toward cost savings, and, therefore, toward profitability.

Let's say you are the financial vice president of a toy manufacturing firm, and the company is contemplating the national introduction of two different computer games. The alternatives are:

1. Produce and market only Test Product LX, supported by a $2 mil-lion marketing effort

2. Produce and market only Test Product LY, supported by a $3 mil-lion marketing effort

3. Produce and market both test products, supported by a $4 million marketing effort

Obviously, the costs that would result from each alternative action are dis-similar. This criterion must embrace the relative profitability of the three options in terms of dollars, i.e., maximization of long-range profits. And if that's too tough to predict, then the vice-president settles for the short-range picture.

In brief, diverse-cost decisions usually call for monetary criteria, those that require a measurement of sales or revenue or costs that can be trans-lated into profitability.

There are, of course, outside factors that influence our choice of criteria. If, for example, the organization is going through a particularly lean period, and cannot afford a large up-front investment, selections might be made purely on the strength of low cost. Using initial cost criteria only, newspaper print advertising might be chosen over a full multimedia campaign, even though the campaign would bring in longer-term profits. Speed, too, might be a reason for selecting one criteria over another. Though a company may prefer to choose an option on the basis of long-term profitability forecasts, there may not be enough time to collect all the necessary data. Surrogate criteria could be more speedily applied.

As we have seen, the benefits in picking the "best" criterion to be used for evaluating alternatives are difficult to quantify. The risks involved in choosing the wrong criteria are also hard to predict. The best guideline we can offer is to keep in mind the key company objective—usually maximizing socially acceptable profit—and select the criteria that can be most closely correlated to this. After that, grit your teeth and make an educated guess.

6

ROLE
OF LOGIC

L ittle did the Greek philosopher Aristotle realize back in 350 B.C. that he would be contributing to your decision making some 2000 plus years later. But if you are serious about working the DMP to your advantage, you and he will be joining forces in maximizing your firm's long-range profits or performance.

Aristotle believed logic played a role in everyday decision making. That's where you and he can get together and exchange notes. Of course

Aristotle thinks of you as a rational animal, prepared to employ reasoning in all its forms. But you and I know better. Much of our action stems from instinct, impulse, whim, and caprice. Ego and insecurities play their parts.

In business decision making, though, it becomes essential that we consciously strive to base our decisions on objective criteria, removing ourselves from irrationality. Call it the scientific method if you wish. This means that logic must enter into our decision making. Employing logic is actually fun. It has been called an "umambiguous language, comprising the rules that thinking must impose upon itself in order to be effective. By and large, logic provides a capacity for distinguishing truth from error when facts or factual data are established. It is the science of proof. The logical man insists that if you claim you have proved a point—about anything at all—then your proof should be scrutinized in terms of your evidence. Logic shows how to make this scrutiny."[1] Competitive business decision making requires this logical approach.

· ·
Inductive and Deductive Thinking

Being rational in our thinking makes the employment of logic in the decision-making process an enjoyable experience. We get the feeling that we are being precise in what we do. Our decisions are based on reasoning, one of the vital elements of logic.

To reason is to take one statement as a *reason* for another. Thus, two statements are necessary if we are to engage in reasoning. For example, your company surveys a sample of U.S. families on ownership of camcorders. One half of the sample state they own camcorders. Therefore, 50 percent of the U.S. families own camcorders.

That is called inductive reasoning, and at this stage Aristotle would be proud of us. Induction simply means that you examine certain data or information and then generalize from that information. The camcorder

----
1. Lionel Ruby, *The Art of Making Sense,* J. B. Lippincott Co., Philadelphia, 1954, p. 23

survey is an example of inductive reasoning. But beware! Your conclusion could be wrong because inductive reasoning often involves the dangerous *inductive leap,* where a generalization goes beyond what was observed. The survey showed that 50 percent owned camcorders. It does not follow that *precisely* 50 percent of U.S. families do in fact own camcorders. The true figure could be 40 percent, or 60 percent, or somewhere in between.

Of course the camcorder data and the subsequent generalization could have some value even though there is quite a spread between 40 and 60 percent. You could call it a *probable truth.* Inductive reasoning's real worth to decision makers centers around its realism. It is operational. You can use it in the decision-making process to reach conclusions that are probably true.

In the deductive argument, Aristotle tells us, if the reason is true (or assumed to be true), then the conclusion necessarily follows. Thus the oldie: "If A, then B." For example, a new stamping machine will reduce stamped parts costs by 20 percent or more; therefore, this operation in the plant will be more cost effective. Of course, you can argue that a new stamping machine will not reduce costs by 20 percent. In that event you would reject the conclusion. But, *if you accept the reason given,* (that costs will be reduced 20 percent or more), then you must agree on the conclusion.

Now that we understand how inductive and deductive thinking work, let's apply this to business decision making. Consider again the "if A, then B" pattern of reasoning. This conditional (or hypothetical) statement is labeled a *syllogism,* because it forms a conditional argument, made up of a premise and a conclusion. The first part of the syllogism is the conditional statement (or the *antecedent*); the second part is the conclusion (or the *consequent*). This "if . . . then" approach is hypothetical, because the "if" phrase is not necessarily a certainty. Let's look at an example:

> IF our firm can sell 500,000 or more units annually of our Special Product KR for five years, THEN we will market the product nationally.

The antecedent is hypothetical: we do not yet know whether we can sell 500,000 units. However, if we know for sure (or are quite certain) that we can sell the 500,000, we then have a truth (or, at least, a probable truth). When the decision makers agree on the truth (or probable truth) of the antecedent, then the consequent must logically follow from the antecedent. In other words, we would roll out the product nationally.

In sum, *when you can reduce the uncertainty of the antecedent to a level acceptable to the decision makers, then the consequent logically becomes a course of action.*

....

Enter: The Criterion

Now that you and Aristotle have joined forces in the decision-making process, let us "re-inject" the decision criterion into the procedure. You will recall the earlier stages of the DMP:

1. Adjustment to new environments

2. Formation of alternatives

3. Selection of criteria

All we have to do now is fit the criteria and alternatives into a conditional syllogism. Remember, always, that to arrive at this stage of the DMP you must have agreement among the decision makers on the precise phrasing of the alternatives, as well as complete accord on the criteria. If your group still insists on debating the nature of the decision options or the specifics of the criteria, move them back to those earlier stages of the DMP until all are prepared to move forward in likeminded fashion.

So let's work the agreed-upon *alternatives* and the selected *criterion* into the conditional statement. The antecedent, the hypothetical "if" clause, as you know, should contain the criterion. The consequent—the "then" phrase—will embrace one of the alternative courses of action.

An example. A manufacturing company has developed two alternative courses of action:

1. Market Special Product KR nationally

2. Do not market special Product KR nationally

These are the only two options being considered. The criteria selected for evaluation is sales, or more specifically, the company decides that a sales level of 500,000 units annually is necessary to justify the decision to enter the national market. The two decision alternatives can be reformulated to include this criteria:

1. IF our firm can sell 500,000 units of Special Product KR annually for five years, THEN we will market the product nationally.

2. IF our firm cannot sell 500,000 units of Special Product KR annually for five years, THEN we will not market the product nationally.

In this way, the selected criteria introduces a specific and clear-cut performance objective into each of the decision alternatives. It will now be much easier to isolate which alternative will better contribute to overall goals.

Of course, everything at this stage is still very "iffy." To return to the example, there is no assurance that 500,000 units can be sold annually. But at least the taskforce making the decision has agreed that if 500,000 units can be sold, then the proposed action will go ahead. Obviously, should a sufficient number of the committee feel that or be able to prove that the 500,000 figure cannot be reached, the national roll-out will not take place.

"I'm a pragmatist, Leon. Before I put a new product on the market, I ask myself, 'Will it sell?'"

Drawing by Weber. © 1986 The New Yorker Magazine, Inc.

Let's take another simple illustration. An advertiser of a new brand of laundry detergent wishes to choose between advertising copy Theme *A* and Theme *B*. As the direct effect of advertising on sales of new products is difficult to forecast, the criterion selected to evaluate the two options is the positive effect each is likely to have on consumer attitude. More specifically, the theme that will make consumers most likely to buy the product will be chosen.

Prior market research has shown that women between the ages of 25 and 45 represent the bulk of the purchases in this product class. Their families are large and they are willing to try out new products. This, then, is the chosen market segment at which the advertising will be targeted.

The alternatives must be reformulated so that the objective is clearly stated in each.

1. IF women in the 25–45 age bracket are more likely to buy the laundry detergent after viewing Theme *A* advertising than after viewing Theme *B* advertising, THEN we will use Theme *A*.

2. IF women in the 25–45 age bracket are more likely to buy the laundry detergent after viewing Theme *B* advertising than after viewing Theme *A* advertising, THEN we will use Theme *B*.

Note again, that this new statement of alternatives also implies what research should be carried out or what new information should be obtained before the alternatives are evaluated.

Note also that because in this example the potential effects of each course of action can be directly compared, this constitutes a *comparative criteria* statement.

Identifying a Critical Point

There is a significant difference between the first and second examples above. The criterion used to evaluate the Special Product KR alternatives states that at least 500,000 units must be sold annually for the decision maker to move ahead. The 500,000 units sales objective is the *critical point* that dictates whether further action is taken. If decision making is to proceed speedily, it is essential that all decision makers involved agree in advance on setting a critical point. If agreement is not reached, this might be a sign that the decision be delayed until more information is obtained.

Let's look at another example that highlights the importance of establishing a critical point. You are the head of a chemical firm in a city with a population of 250,000. There have been unfounded rumors among local residents that fumes have been escaping from your plant, endangering public health. You have looked into this and know beyond any doubt there is no truth in the rumors. Yet, you are concerned because you wish your firm to be considered a good member of the community.

To bolster the company's image and to counter the rumor, you consider running a series of advertisements in the local newspaper. Others in the organization feel that this is not necessary; the rumor will die down in time. Thus the alternatives are:

1. Run a series of public interest advertisements

2. Do not run the advertisements

Improving public opinion of the organization is the criterion chosen for evaluating these alternatives. Without further defining the evaluation criterion, and without setting a critical point, you authorize a survey to determine public opinion on the fumes issue. The survey reveals that ten percent of residents claim it is a serious problem. "Just as I said," pronounces one manager, "There's nothing to worry about." But another executive retorts, "What do you mean? Ten percent of residents can't be ignored. That's a lot of people!"

And so a debate ensues, all because you did not formulate a criteria statement and agree on the critical point. This could have been avoided if you had decided in advance of the survey what degree of dissatisfaction among residents would warrant running the advertising. The issue could have been resolved quickly and peacefully.

Before we wind up our discussion of criteria selection, let's look at a real-life business example that involves high financial risk. The company is USX Corp., formerly the U.S. Steel Corporation. In 1990, as the company's largest shareholder with more than 13 percent of USX stock, Carl Icahn outlined options the organization could take to improve its chances of survival. These can be summarized as:

1. Allocate funds for modernizing plants

2. Merge with another firm

3. Sell off designated plants and restrict marketing efforts to a reduced, more profitable line of products

This, quite obviously, is a high-risk, strategic, financial decision. As the cost involved in effecting any of the three alternatives varies considerably, it is a diverse-cost decision. The criterion selected needs to center on potential for enhancing the future long-range profits of the organization. Here is a statement that reformulates the three options, incorporating this criterion:

> IF one of the three options being considered maximizes long-range profits more than the other two, THEN we will choose that alternative.

The situation changes dramatically if we add a fourth option: none of the above three. In other words, the decision makers feel that the door should be open to reject all three, and take no action at all. This fourth option makes it necessary to set a critical point to further define the first three options. In this way, if none of the three alternatives can produce a minimum stated profit (established by the critical point), then none of the three will be taken.

Remember that even once our selection criteria have been agreed upon and possible courses of action have been reformulated to clarify the point at which action will be taken, we are still in the pre-decisional phase of the decision-making process. No positive action has been taken—all our options are still open. We have progressed, however, to the point at which we have a clear-cut and objective means of evaluating different alternatives so that we can confidently select one above the others. This is the subject of the next chapter.

7

SELECTING
THE BEST
ALTERNATIVE

It has been said before, and here it is again: making a decision entails making a prediction. This is your criterion: IF we can sell 500,000 or more units a year for the next five years, THEN we will market Special Product KR. All *you* have to do is predict whether your firm will sell 500,000 units or more annually. If the answer is yes, then you will opt for marketing the item. If you predict that the company cannot sell 500,000, then you will give it the *No Go* sign. It's that simple. Or is it?

We are now at the actionable phase of the decision-making process: the making of a prediction based on the criteria statement agreed upon earlier in the DMP by you and others in your group. (This is the antecedent, the "if . . ." side of the conditional criteria formulation.)

The issue at the moment is whether you and the others on your committee can agree on proceeding with Special Product KR. In other words, is your prediction readily accepted as being sufficiently accurate to justify your firm marketing your Product KR? If there is agreement among the decision makers, you raise the green *GO* flag and charge forward.

If there is disagreement, do you junk the KR project? Not at all. Disagreement simply means that you may choose to delay making the decision at this moment so that more and better information and possibly expert opinion can be gathered, thus reducing the disagreement on whether to proceed with Special Product KR. This is the *actionable data* that will aid you in taking action, i.e., selecting one alternative over the others for implementation.

This is where analysis goes out the window. Remember, you are not operating in a closed, self-contained world of certainty. You, as a decision maker, must now rely on an educated guess. No number crunchers spring to your aid to tell you whether to delay or proceed now. Putting off making the decision would reduce the lead time over your competition. If you delay, your competitors may learn of your plans and jump the gun on you, resulting in a loss of sales and revenue that you could have gained during the period of delay.

So why delay? Why not flex your muscles and either market Special Product KR, or forget it—right now? Here, in two parts, is the governing rule:

You postpone making the decision . . .

1. When the level of disagreement among the decision makers runs high, and . . .

2. When the profit consequences of a wrong decision are great.

Assessing the extent of the decision makers' agreement and disagreement is a tough first step.

. . . .

Determining Level of Agreement/Disagreement

If you are the lone decision maker in your organization, the decision on whether to delay or proceed with one of the stated alternatives is determined by the uncertainty in your own mind. This may lead to your delaying the decision so that you can obtain more information or expert opinion on what direction to go.

However, in consensus decision making, as a member of a committee or task force, you recognize group-uncertainty by observing the disagreement level among the decision makers. Obviously, when *agreement* exists, scant uncertainty is present: The decision criterion has been formulated, the prediction made, and the decision makers agree.

The situation becomes thorny when *disagreement* sets in. How, then, can you determine whether the disagreement level is high enough to dictate delay? As mentioned above, you can sense it by heeding the nature of the discussion. Heated comments and verbal thrusts attest to a high level of disagreement. ("How can you guys *possibly* say we should go ahead with KR when you know and I know the product is both over-priced and unacceptable to the market? Anyone who says we should market this thing is stupid!")

But some discussions are softer, without carping, rebuke, or cavil. Thoughtful comments combined with the employment of formal logic serve as the basis of the deliberations. ("Although some of you may not agree, I feel that our sales people have gone on record as strongly favoring this product. They insist, and I agree with them, that we can attain a 500,000 sales level.")

Disagreement exists among the decision makers in both of the above examples; only the nature of the discussion is different. In assessing the level of disagreement you can sometimes *sense* whether a delay is desirable. Or, you can attempt to *measure* the disagreement level by asking the committee members to scale their opinions on whether to take action now or delay. This measurement can be achieved by submitting a written form to the decision makers, asking them to assess their feelings on a ten point scale regarding the alternative courses of actions being discussed.

The form would look something like this:

Do Not Market Product KR				Not Sure				Market Product KR Now	
1	2	3	4	5	6	7	8	9	10

Let's say there are five members in your group, including yourself. You gather the five responses and list them:

Person	Scale
A	2
B	8
C	3
D	7
E	5

Quantifying the responses reveals an arithmetic average score of 5.0, suggesting that the group opposes the move by the slightest of margins (the midpoint is technically 5.5). But more important than the 5.0 score is the great disagreement exhibited on what action to take. Two members of the group (A and C responding 2 and 3) strongly oppose placing the product on the market while two others (B and D responding 7 and 8) vigorously favor going ahead at this time. A decision delay would appear to be in order in light of the dissimilar views on the issue.

Let's look at a different set of figures. Assume the decision makers scaled their feelings as 7, 8, 7, 8, and 10. Here, obviously, high agreement prevails, resulting in a score of 8.0. On the basis of this figure a *GO* would be dictated.

Now, let's assume the five committee people scaled their thinking in this manner: 5, 5, 6, 6, and 5. Virtual agreement? Not really. True, all scales cluster around the mid-ground levels of 5 or 6. There appears to be no disagreement. Now what do you do? Go ahead with Special Product KR, reject it, or delay the decision? The scale data reveal a lack of strong feeling—one way or the other. Each member of your group is, in essence, saying that he or she is still struggling with whether to move in the *GO* or *NO GO* direction. In other words, there is a high level of uncertainty—a shared doubt, let us say—and, as we know, *disagreement among decision*

"*That makes four 'Yes'es and one 'No, no, a thousand times no.'*"

Drawing by Vietor; © 1982, The New Yorker Magazine, Inc.

makers emerges from uncertainty. Clearly, what the decision makers are saying is that they agree that they are uncertain as to what to do; they disagree with anybody who says that the answer is obvious.

Disagreement, then, requires a decision *delay* so that more and/or better information can be gathered. *Agreement,* where the decision makers cluster around either a positive or negative point, results in action, i.e., making the decision *without delay.*

But wait! Don't jump too quickly.

What about Profit Consequences?

Having a high level of agreement is not the sole determinant of whether to take action at this point of the DMP. It is necessary also to judge the potential damage that could result from a "wrong" decision being made (the second part of the "governing rule" mentioned on page 72.)

The amount of money involved does not always suggest a high level of profit consequences. Imagine, for example, that you are a municipal bond buyer for a large financial institution. You have $1,000,000 to invest and have narrowed your purchase alternatives down to two issues recently offered. Both are general obligation bonds, and have identical triple A ratings by Moody's and Standard and Poor. They are offered by the same state, have the same credit rating, mature in the same year, and both are callable eight years down the road. Although the investment is high—$1,000,000—the consequences of making a wrong decision are minimal. Either bond would benefit the purchaser to the same extent, with virtually the same amount of risk.

Here is another set of alternatives, also involving a $1,000,000 investment. The Red Catsup Company is considering changing the label on its Red 'n Thick brand and the changeover is estimated to cost $1,000,000. The current label has been used successfully for 19 years, but management feels the logotype is no longer in keeping with the image now being developed by the firm. So, a new Red 'n Thick label has been designed. The alternatives are:

1. Adopt a new label

2. Stay with the old label

Sales revenue is the evaluation criterion.

In this example, the consequences of a wrong decision are great. Not only is the initial $1,000,000 investment at stake, but should the new logo be unsuccessful, a sales decline could result, leading to further losses. In assessing the consequences of the label change, then, the decision makers must strike a happy balance between risk taking and risk aversion. Their agreement/disagreement level, combined with an assessment of the profit consequences, provides them with a final basis for determining the need for a decision delay.

. . . .

Level of Agreement and Profit Consequences

These two components—agreement level and consequences on profitability—can be merged into a grid that will graphically portray the need for delay. The simple diagram in Exhibit 7.1 indicates when to postpone the decision and when to move forward without delay.

It is obvious from the grid that anytime you have high agreement you move forward with the decision. You *ACT NOW.* There is no reason to

---

EXHIBIT 7.1   A grid for determining when to delay a decision

	High Agreement	High Disagreement
High Profit Consequences	ACT NOW	DELAY
Low Profit Consequences	ACT NOW	ACT NOW

---

delay, regardless of the perceived profit consequences of a wrong decision. You have the group's agreement and more data presumably would not change the thinking of the committee members. So why delay?

When there is high disagreement on the decision options, involving a low level of risk, you should move ahead anyway. You could be right. And even if you make the wrong decision, the consequences are minimal. Delay would gain little or nothing and would only cost you money and would postpone the benefits that might result from taking action now. Besides, implementing a decision now will provide the best possible additional data. The actual consequences of your decision can trigger a new and more successful round of the decision-making process.

This leaves us with a blend of high disagreement and high-profit consequences. This is when you delay, seeking more information or expert opinion. The consequences are too great to risk making a wrong decision, so you hold back and gather more data aimed at reducing the chances of your going in the wrong direction.

People vs. Numbers

In this chapter, we have talked about the need for personal judgment in the decision-making process. Pick up almost any book on decision making and the immediate impression it makes is that numbers alone can dictate the rules of decision making. How wrong this is! Quantitative analysis is fine, but don't forget that decisions are made by people and, therefore, the

"All those in favor . . . ."

better you understand people and the ways they think, the better you will become at decision making.

To help you, let's round off the chapter by taking a look at the types of individuals you can expect to meet in the decision-making process. Notice how your understanding of people can introduce different variables that affect the ways decisions are made.

First, look at the level of *experience* of each of the people in a particular decision-making group. Suppose that in making a decision, five committee members scale their level of agreement to a certain course of action as follows: 2, 3, 5, 7, and 8. The average score is 5.00, indicating a high level of uncertainty which calls for a delay and the gathering of more information. But don't rely solely on the numbers—look at who these five people are and notice how they compare in terms of experience. The two members who scale at 2 and 3 (in opposition) could be the company president and executive vice president who, combined, have a total of 40 years experience in the business. Those who scale heavily in favor at 7 and 8 might have only eight years experience between them. The point is that you should consider each person's judgment in terms of his or her experience.

Let's see how this works. Should you give equal weight to all five members of the group? Hardly. You may decide to assign triple weight to the president and vice president. This, would, of course, affect the outcome of the discussion greatly. The scaling information, tempered by a consideration of level of experience would now look like this: 2, (2), (2), 3, (3), (3), 5, 7, and 8. The overall score would be $35/9$, which gives a lower average score of 3.9. Instead of uncertainty, you now have a clear disagreement to the proposed course of action. Bland allegiance to numbers, can, therefore, mislead. A personal judgment is needed to make the right decision.

Another characteristic to look for in the participants of any group meeting is *insecurity*. All of us are insecure or lacking in confidence at one time or another. This is all the more common when the boss participates in meetings. In our desire to impress, we are tempted to set aside our own judgments and follow the boss, holding fast to any opinion he or she supports. "Boss supporters" like this can heavily weight a discussion in one direction—once the boss voices an opinion, the boss supporters back it up and meaningful arguments are unheard. Too frequently, the boss' opinion prevails.

Another insecure type is the *egocentric*, who sees everything from a single, self-interested point of view. How would the adoption of one alternative over others affect *my* role within the company? Would it make *me* look good? Would it mean extra work? Would it enhance or curb *my* position? Frequently, egocentrics are the most verbose members of a committee—they strive to cover up real feelings and motivations with an excess of words.

In most meetings, too, you should be able to identify at least one participant who stubbornly sticks to one point of view and refuses even to consider others. This is the *stone-waller* who, having publicly stated his or her opinion, refuses to listen to or be influenced by other suggestions. This attitude again displays insecurity—too deep a belief that to change one's mind publicly is an admission of failure. Unlike the stone-waller, a mature decision maker has the confidence to recant under the glare of peers and superiors and opt for the best possible course of action.

As the chairperson you face the job of determining how to handle these varied persons. No rule applies, but you will recall the Chapter 1 discussion on the role of persuasiveness in decision making.

Observing the stances people take in meetings can, then, tell you a great deal about their motivations for backing one alternative or for arguing against another. To improve your own performance in group discussions and to contribute more to decision making, find out as much as you can about the other participants. When evaluating their opinions, consider the breadth of their experience, their roles within the organization, and the reasons they may have for supporting or rejecting different decision options. By all means use quantifiable techniques—such as the agreement/disagreement scale—in evaluating alternatives, but remember, that personal opinions and judgments count. Remember, too, the importance of the educated guess.

8

GATHERING
ACTIONABLE
DATA

W hen you delay making a decision, you do so because you and the
other decision makers involved have agreed that new, actionable
data or expert opinion are needed to reduce the chances of making the
wrong choice. All this data collection takes place while the main issue is on
hold.

You are now within one or more mini-decision structures—the
"wheels-within-a-wheel" we identified at the end of Chapter 2. The

mini-decisions you need to make may be, for example, what method should be employed in gathering new data, how much time should be set aside for conducting a survey, or how responsibilities and funds should be assigned for carrying out information-gathering tasks. Each of these mini-decisions is, itself, a candidate for the decision-making process, and for each you will need to go through the same phases: developing alternatives, setting evaluation criteria, and choosing one of the options posed.

Let's look at the factors that should be considered when the decision makers opt to put a decision on hold and enter one or more mini-decision cycles.

. . . .
Determining What Actionable Data Are Needed

The obvious starting point for the delay phase of the DMP is determining what actionable data or information are required. It is easy to gloss over this rather specialized area of decision making with such phrases as "gather the appropriate data" or "collect information that will improve our chances of making the right decision." But this is much too vague. What is meant by "appropriate" or "improve our chances"? *In highly specific terms,* exactly what new information should we be seeking?

The best way to answer this is to go back to the criterion statements you made earlier in the decision-making process. To illustrate, let's look again at the criterion statement we selected for Special Product KR in Chapter 6:

IF our firm can sell 500,000 units of Special Product KR annually for five years, THEN we will market the product nationally.

In this example, the decision makers cannot agree on whether a sales level (a critical point) of 500,000 units can reasonably be achieved and, therefore, opt to gather some new actionable data before a final course of action is chosen. Notice how the criterion statement itself tells us what new information we need—to reduce the uncertainty among the decision makers.

Let's assume Special Product KR is an industrial rather than a consumer product, such as, for example, a newly-designed hospital bed. To test market whether the criterion statement is achievable would require the exceedingly costly effort of producing the product and marketing the product for a good number of months, and then saying: ''It looks great!'' or ''We sure bombed out on that one!'' That is just what you are attempting to avoid: the high cost of getting into the actual business of producing and marketing the product, only to discover to your embarrassment that you bombed out.

What is needed in this instance is a surrogate criterion, closely related to sales. You would drop the ''unit sales'' in the ''IF'' clause of the criteria statement, substituting a different criterion you feel approximates a prediction of sales. On hospital beds, for example, a properly conducted survey of hospital purchasing agents could measure the degree of the customers' stated ''likelihood of buying'' the new product, comparing it to existing products on the market. Knowing the magnitude of the annual hospital bed market, and the share now obtained by your competition, it would be feasible to compute what share of the market you could garner— based on how well Special Product KR stacks up alongside competition. If this figure were 500,000 units or more, you would roll out the product nationally.

It is essential, then, to tailor your criteria to the nature of your product, employing a surrogate when necessary. And that means often.

Let's look at another example. A mid-sized bank in a mid-sized community needs to decide whether or not it should open a new branch office within the community. Before making the decision, the management wants to be sure that a designated profit point will be reached. If the decision makers agree that it is possible to achieve a given profit level by opening a new branch, then the expansion will go ahead. If not, the idea will be dropped.

As in the previous example, setting a critical point is useful in specifying exactly what new information is needed. If the critical point criterion is to achieve, for example, up to $2,000,000 weekly in commercial deposits from businesses in the community at the new branch office, this indicates that the new information needed will concern details such as the weekly turnovers of local businesses, or details on the banks at which local businesses currently hold their accounts. If the critical point criterion is to attract 50 new personal accounts to the branch each month, the new information needed is more likely to concern demographics of the people in the community, such as their ages, family make-up, level of income, etc.

Again, the criterion statement indicates the *type* of information we need, and the critical point tells us *how specific* that information should be.

Experimental Data

Experimental data are those that result from setting up "experiments" to estimate (or predict) the impact of decision options. Let's look at an example.

You are considering increasing the retail price of a grocery food item in your line. The brand is a leading contributor to profit, so any tampering with its price is risky. You decide to delay the decision until you obtain information upon which accurate predictions can be made.

An experiment is set up whereby you measure the cause and effect relationship of the price change. In designing the experiment, you seek to control all variables except the one you are measuring: the price change. Such factors as distribution, shelf facings, shelf positions, and competitive promotional and merchandising activities are held constant (or randomized). In this way the consequence of your price change—within the known limits of survey error—can be identified. Thus, the cause and effect relationship is determined, i.e. you can predict the impact of the price change on sales, revenue, and profit. If the sales (or revenue or profit) reach the critical point designated in the criterion statement, then you proceed to adjust your price accordingly.

Experimental data are not easy to come by, and should be assembled by researchers and statisticians fully versed in the techniques of conducting surveys. This is especially true of experiments aimed at measuring the behavior of people, in contrast, say, to more easily quantifiable experiments, such as those conducted to measure quality control or other operational procedures in the manufacturing process. Later in this chapter we will look in more detail at some of the drawbacks of relying on the results of surveys in making decisions.

••

Cost of Collecting Actionable Data

Once you have determined exactly what type of actionable data you need, the next task is to decide how much you are prepared to spend on collecting it. One theory is that the cost of finding information should not exceed the estimated profit consequences of a wrong decision. Thus, if a wrong decision could cause your firm to lose $100,000, you can justify spending up to this amount in pursuit of data that would preclude your making that wrong decision. But this theory doesn't always work in practice, particularly when the investments at risk are high. Let's assume your firm stands to lose $2 million by making a wrong decision. You could spend up to $2 million for data aimed at avoiding that decision, but common sense tells us that this is too much money to spend where the loss, without the data, would, in any case, approach that amount.

A far better way of deciding how much to spend on data is to determine first how accurate and how useful those data should be. Basically, the higher the level of disagreement among decision makers and the greater the risk involved, the more accurate the data should be. If, for example, the proposed introduction of Special Product KR risks millions of corporate dollars, and if the decision on whether to proceed brings on heated discussions, then a thorough study, resulting in highly precise actionable data is justified. In contrast, a decision on whether to print the corner card of an envelope light blue or dark blue involves minimum risk and, let's say, only mild differences of opinion. Thus, a high-cost survey is not in order—the advice of a color consultant would suffice.

In essence, then, deciding on how accurate information should be and at what cost it should be obtained, depends on the judgment of the decision makers. It has to be an educated guess.

The time available for the collection of actionable data also influences and often dictates the amount of money that is spent. For example, for a detailed consumer attitude survey to be conducted within weeks or even days, the cost will be high. One can argue about the worth of time-pressured studies, for there is a high level of risk in relying on surveys made in days when weeks or months should have been allowed. Inaccurate information can turn up from such hurried surveys, and they can, therefore, lead to wrong decisions. Thus, the cost of such data becomes great when measured in terms of the decision consequences. The other side of the argument is that it is better to have *some* data, on which to base decisions, albeit hastily collected. Again, this is a judgment call for the decision makers. Another educated guess.

There is one further cost factor to consider: opportunity cost. The mere delay, in itself, can be detrimental to the organization's profitability. When decision makers move into a holding pattern while actionable data are collected, an opportunity for sales and revenue or for reduced costs is lost. Of course, the delay may be the right move, but at a price.

As you can see, then, determining the total costs involved in delaying a decision and funding further research is complex. Before you decide to delay, make sure you have been realistic in your assessment of the decision makers' agreement levels and the profit consequences of a wrong decision.

· ·

When Data Mislead

No matter how honest or objective we try to be, and no matter how carefully we collect the information on which to base decisions, the way in which we handle data can sometimes distort or mislead. Whether you are collecting data yourself or are entrusting that job to others, always remember that the data you see may be distorted.

Let's look at some of the ways in which the techniques we use for collecting and interpreting data can trick us.

Beware the Sample Survey

Sample surveys are a common technique used in collecting actionable data. Before you authorize a survey, make sure you know *who* is to be sampled and *what sampling procedures* will be used. The examples below illustrate these two points.

Who is being sampled?

Ugottem University wants to impress its alumni and others by showing how successful its graduates are. So, the university conducts a survey. The results look great. The news story in the alumni magazine touts: ''Ugottem University Alumni Earn $150,000 a Year within Five Years of Graduation.''

But how do we know this story is reliable? It doesn't tell us who was surveyed. Ugottem graduates? Yes, but that's all we know. The survey was conducted by mail. But how many of the original sample did not respond, and who were they? If I were a recent Ugottem graduate, penniless and out of a job, I would not have returned the questionnaire. I have pride! However, if I were making $200,000 a year, you can be sure I would have been delighted to provide the surveyors with my information.

More than that, people who are down on their luck move often and are difficult to locate. They don't leave forwarding addresses. They may *want* to get lost. The last thing they need is a letter from some Ugottem group seeking a contribution of $25,000.

In a broad sense, mail surveys are suspect, because with a low response rate you encounter difficulty in determining the differences between those who did and those who did not return the questionnaire. This means you do not have an acceptable handle on the nature of your sample. In other words, you do not know who was *really* surveyed. True, those who responded were surveyed, but do they accurately represent the situations or opinions of those who did not reply?

Mail surveys, however, are not all bad. Those with a high response rate can be very reliable. Moreover, as any survey expert you consult can tell you, there are various devices that can be employed to increase response rates.

Telephone surveys tend to be criticized for similar reasons: They do not provide data on those who are not reached by telephone, or on those who refuse interviews. In recent years, though, this interviewing approach has shown to be highly reliable with the employment of sophisticated computerized sample-selection procedures. Also, conducting a survey by telephone results in a far less expensive study than the personal interview method propounded long ago by the famous Dr. George Gallup. However, even the telephone survey is coming under fire. With the advent of telemarketing and the resultant growth of public resistance to a claimed invasion of privacy, the legitimate telephone survey may be an innocent victim—telephone subscribers are not able to differentiate between telemarketing and the true survey. This results in a greater refusal rate among respondents, thus detracting to some extent from the reliability of the telephone survey sample.

Are the samples really comparable?

Another problem with sample surveys is that they often claim to make comparisons between groups that are simply not comparable. Frequently, for example, we read about how much a college education is worth to individuals. Surveys have claimed that if you go to college, you will make "on the average" $500,000 more during a lifetime than your counterpart who did not obtain a college education. The survey technique used is a comparison of college graduates' incomes with those of non-graduates.

The weakness in this technique is that no variables other than college background are used. The survey makes assumptions based solely on level of education. It overlooks the fact that the two groups are two completely different types of people. The college-bound are, perhaps, more likely to have been bright, imaginative, and hard-working students in high school. That is why they were admitted to college in the first place. They may also have attended more academically-oriented high schools. This group, then, is certainly more likely to secure better jobs and earn more money, but the fact that they "went away to school" is not the sole reason. If they had not gone to college, they most likely would have earned more in later life.

To determine the reliability of the sample surveyed, ask this one question: Does the sampling unit (a person, a stamped part, a place of accounting data) have an *equal or known* chance of being included in the sample? If the answer is yes, you are on the right track. If not, find out why not.

Are you getting information, even when your sample meets the necessary requirements?

We all want people to think well of us. I don't go out of my way to tell my friends of my many inadequacies. If an interviewer were to ask me what publications I *read*, I could answer honestly: *The Wall Street Journal, Business Week,* and *Mayo Clinic Health Letter.* In my subconscious desire to "look good" in front of the interviewer I probably would not mention the magazines I read in the barber shop waiting room. In other words, the mere asking of a question does not guarantee an accurate response.

The sequence and phrasing of questions have profound impact on the reliability of data. In one survey with which I was involved, one question was posed very early in the questionnaire: I requested the respondent's overall attitude toward a particular service. The findings showed 84 percent had "very favorable" attitudes. Then, as an experiment with a matched sample of persons, the same question was placed near the end of the questionnaire. It followed various queries about the good and bad points of the service being surveyed. The "very favorable" attitude dropped to 55 percent after respondents had been reminded of some of the weakness in the service. Which of those two percentages is the more reliable? Probably somewhere between those two extremes. Sophisticated questionnaire development could have narrowed that range considerably.

Ad-man Bruce Barton once said, "Everybody thinks he can write a questionnaire!" How true. But few people turn out to be good at it. If you are inexperienced in survey techniques, don't be tempted to write your own questionnaire. In the long term, it will pay to bring in the professionals. As far back as 1972 George Gallup wrote in his *The Sophisticated Poll Watcher's Guide* that "Nothing is so difficult, nor so important, as the selection and wording of questions." If your information is based on questionnaire findings, get professional help. It isn't nearly so much the cost of obtaining wasteful data as it is the profit consequences of your making a bad decision based on incorrect information. That could be *really* costly!

Don't rely on accuracy claims

One of the common elements of news stories (and business reports) based on polls is the qualifying statement that the data are "accurate within this or that percent." Our local newspaper in a recent issue ran stories covering three separate polls; here are the qualifying statements:

1. "Of those who heard the president's speech, 40 percent agreed with the president while 49 percent opposed his view. The poll had a margin of error of plus or minus five percentage points."

2. "Thirty-eight percent said relations with the Soviet Union had improved under the current administration. . . . The results are subject to an error margin of three percentage points either way."

3. ". . . The chances are 95 out of 100 that the survey findings will not vary more than five percentage points plus or minus from the data shown. . . ."

Such statements mis-inform. In all three surveys the true situation could be 20 or 30 percentage points from the published figures. The qualifying statements are really saying that if the survey were repeated immediately, using the same questionnaire and a matched sample, then there is a statistical chance that 95 times out of 100 the published data will not exceed the stated limits.

Take the first example where 40 percent plus or minus five percent agreed with the president. This means, of course, that the "real" figure is somewhere between 45 percent on the plus side and 35 percent on the minus side. But, and here's the crusher, that assumes the questionnaire was perfect, with no bias, that the interviewers followed the questions precisely as they were written, that the answers were recorded with unfailing exactness, that the tabulation of the raw data was 100 percent accurate, and that no errors were introduced in writing the results to the computer.

"OUR LATEST POLL SHOWS THAT 68% OF THE VOTERS THINK THAT 91% OF THE POLLS ARE INACCURATE 71% OF THE TIME -- PLUS OR MINUS THREE PERCENTAGE POINTS."

Source: © 1988. Reprinted with special permission of North America Syndicate, Inc.

When these "accuracy" statements are made, the writer of the report or news story is alluding only to *sampling* error. Ignored are the *non-sampling* errors that very often are greater than those attributed to sampling. The well-known Gallup opinion research firm is one of the few that publicly tempers in meaningful terms the accuracy of its data in its syndicated columns. This is the qualifying statement:

"... For results based on samples this size, one can say with 95 percent confidence that the error attributable to sampling and other random effects could be four percentage points in either direction. In addition to sampling error, the reader should bear in mind that question wording and practical difficulties in conducting surveys can introduce error or bias into the findings of opinion polls."

One more point: The accuracy level of the data is in part related to the percentages produced. For example, an 80–20 percent break in the data is more reliable than a 50–50 split, in terms of margin of error. Also, when you are looking at sub-samples where analysts have used smaller base figures, percentages are usually less reliable than when the total sample is employed.

On balance, view sample survey data with a jaundiced eye. Know the people who conduct the surveys for you. Know whom or what they are sampling. Check the questionnaire and survey techniques used. And notice how the responses or statistics are interpreted.

Averages! Watch 'Em

A sales manager I once knew was eager to recruit a salesman who had a great track record with a competitor. The sales manager was convinced he could attract this young man if the magnitude of the potential earnings were to be made clear. "The average earnings in commissions of my eleven sales people amount to $90,000 per person!" boasted the sales manager. The young candidate was now earning $60,000 and a likely boost to $90,000 or more was appealing indeed. If his critical point criterion was an increase of $30,000 or more, then he would accept the offer.

But the sales manager was using the term "average earnings" in a loose manner. He employed the arithmetic mean in computing the "average." His "average earnings" figure was correct enough, but inappropriate and misleading in this particular case. His eleven salesmen had these earnings:

Salesman	Annual Earnings	
A	$38,000	
B	42,000	
C	47,000	
D	50,000	
E	50,000	
F	53,000	(median)
G	60,000	
H	62,000	
I	64,000	
J	64,000	
K	460,000	

It is obvious that Salesman K either had an uncle in the business or a house account the size of the U.S. Department of Defense. Salesman K has earned an exceptional level of commissions. The arithmetic average for the group was $90,000, as the sales manager claimed. But the *median* commissions figure (where half the salesmen earned less than the middle figure, and half earned more) showed the ''average'' to be $53,000—a far more accurate portrayal than the arithmetic average where all earnings are dumped into one hat and divided by the number of sales people.

Some time ago, a well-known company announced that its employees' ''average'' earnings went up 107 percent over a given eight-year period. Impressive! But it was revealed later that early during the eight-year period the company employed a large number of part-time workers, most of whom then became full timers. Quite obviously, if you work half-time for a couple of years and then move to full time, your earnings just about double. But that doesn't mean that the average wage rate has doubled!

Distorting Graphics

It is tempting to try to look good in front of others. Subconsciously, we seek admiration from our peers and we want our recommendations or ideas to be accepted over others. Temptation can, however, lead us to distort data, sometimes deliberately, sometimes not. Watch yourself and others and analyze your motives to guard against miscoloring data.

The simple graph is often used for data camouflage. In the examples which follow, based on *How to Lie with Statistics,*[1] we will see how graphs can be used to illustrate and support any argument we choose.

Take a simple line graph. You start with the two axes and place the time line along the bottom, and dollars (in millions) up the left hand side. Then you plot changes in revenue from January through December, and draw a line to show a slight upward trend. Your graph—Exhibit 8.1—indicates a 10 percent increase in revenue. Everything appears to be in order, and the entire graph is in proportion, with the zero line at the bottom. With only a passing glance the upward trend is apparent. And if you look at the figures you see a change of 10 percent. This is a pleasant trend, but not overwhelming.

----
1.   Darrell Huff, pictures by Irving Geis. Reproduced with permission of W. W. Norton & Company, Inc. Copyright 1954 Darrell Huff and Irving Geis. Copyright renewed 1982 by Darrell Huff and Irving Geis.

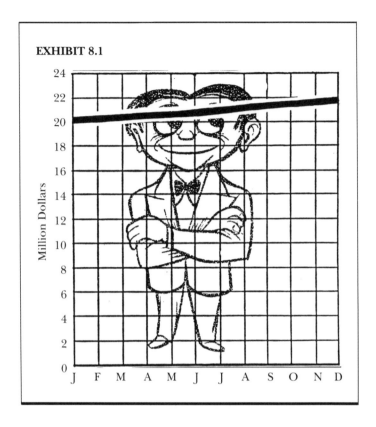

EXHIBIT 8.1

Let's assume you want to make this increase *seem* more dramatic. Using the same graph, you can just cut it down in size and chop it off at the bottom. The picture changes, as in Exhibit 8.2. The numbers are identical to those in the earlier graph, but the dollars appear to have climbed a third of the way up the chart. The increase in revenue is the same, but it *looks* greater.

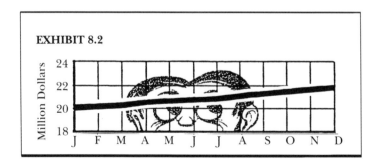

EXHIBIT 8.2

Impressive, not only to the casual observer but to the interested party as well. It looks good, so it must be good! The secret, of course, is to present the chart with a scale that does not start from zero. This artifice exaggerates the moderate increase.

But you can do even better. Just change the proportion between the ordinate and the abscissa. It certainly drives your point home in great style. See it in Exhibit 8.3. The increase now looks a lot more substantial: instead of a measly 10 percent increase, you now have a whopping 10 percent increase!

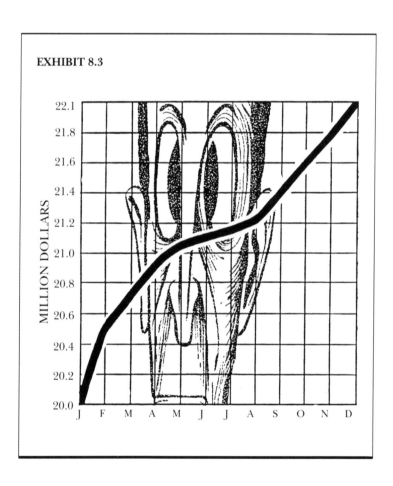

EXHIBIT 8.3

There's no law against playing with graphic representations in this way. It's done all the time. Even the reliable standby *The Wall Street Journal* uses this technique to press home a point (see Exhibit 8.4).

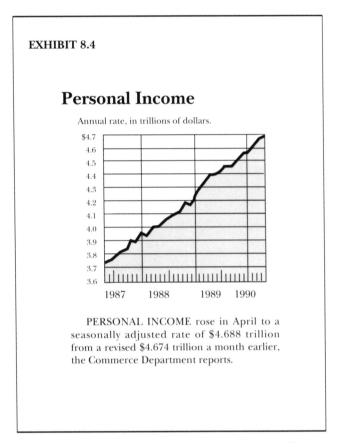

EXHIBIT 8.4

Personal Income

Annual rate, in trillions of dollars.

PERSONAL INCOME rose in April to a seasonally adjusted rate of $4.688 trillion from a revised $4.674 trillion a month earlier, the Commerce Department reports.

Much better, and certainly more faithful in what it reveals, is Exhibit 8.5. This chart by the Scottish Development Agency portrays the complete picture of the growth of cellular phones in Europe without resorting to subtle graphic devices. Everything is in proportion and the zero line is at the bottom.

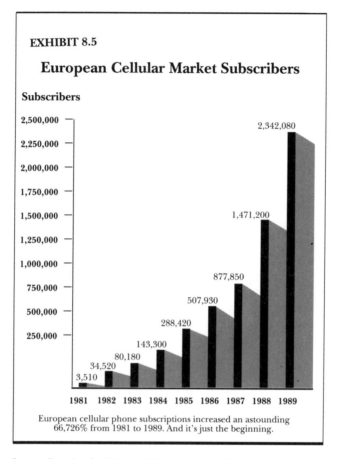

EXHIBIT 8.5

European Cellular Market Subscribers

Subscribers

European cellular phone subscriptions increased an astounding 66,726% from 1981 to 1989. And it's just the beginning.

Source: Reprinted with permission by the Scottish Development Agency, Stamford, CT, and Clarke Goward Fitts Matteson, Boston, MA

Then there is the so-called one-dimensional graphic. Let's say I plan to show a comparison between the weekly wages of workers in Lower Uzeeka and the United States. U.S. workers earn twice as much as their faraway counterparts. This can be portrayed in simple fashion with a bar chart—one bar being twice as tall as the other and both the same width. But a more interesting impression can be created if an artist will come to our aid and draw two men: a U.S. worker standing alongside two bags of dollars, while a Lower Uzeekan has only one. Exhibit 8.6 illustrates this approach.

EXHIBIT 8.6

The graphic is acceptable enough, but you have to search for the main point, which is that the U.S. worker has double the earnings of his distant counterpart. So let's try again. This time, we will provide each worker with just one bag of dollars, but the U.S wage earner's bag will be twice the size.

EXHIBIT 8.7

Now that's more like it! The U.S. bag is twice as big—or is it? It is twice as tall, but *double in width as well.* It occupies *four* times as much space as the poor worker from abroad, a four to one ratio. And that's not all. "Since these are pictures of objects having in reality three dimensions, the second must be twice as thick as the first. As your geometry book puts it, the volumes of similar solids vary as the cube of any like dimension. Two times two times two is eight."[2] So, even though one worker makes twice as much as the other, the *impression* is that the American's wage truly dwarfs the foreigner's.

If you locate the right cartographer-statistician combination, you can in all likelihood come up with a chart to support almost any position. In the "Statistics Brief" column of *The Economist* of London, a series of cases was developed showing how one situation can be presented in four different lights.[3] Wrote the columnist:

"Never mind if the data does not fit the argument, a chart will soon prove the point, for example, scales that do not start from zero will exaggerate modest movements, while logarithmic scales can flatten out an increase. . . . Suppose the national union of office cleaners was after a big pay rise, then Chart 1 (Exhibit 8.8) on an ordinary scale would make impressive reading: over the past 10 years, the salary of managing directors appears to have risen much faster than that of office cleaners, and the wage gap has widened. The managing director might offer Chart 2 (on a logarithmic scale) in his defense. This suggests (correctly) that the wages of office cleaners have been rising at a faster pace than his own, and (misleadingly) that the absolute wage gap has narrowed.

"Even so, the absolute gap still looks embarrassingly large. No problem; re-base the figures on to an index (Chart 3) or express them as a percentage change on a year ago (Chart 4)—i.e., pick the chart that suits you best."

----

2. *Ibid.*

3. "Statistics Brief," *The Economist,* London, 31 May, 1986

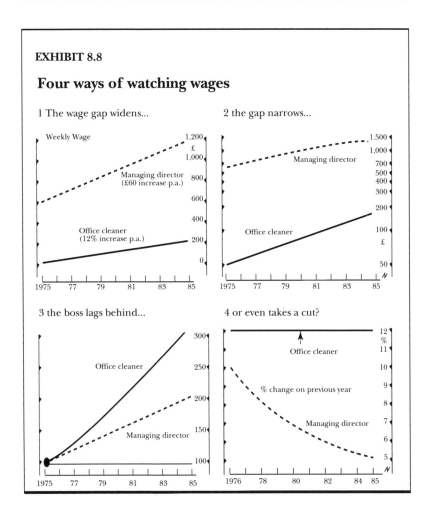

EXHIBIT 8.8

Four ways of watching wages

1 The wage gap widens...

2 the gap narrows...

3 the boss lags behind...

4 or even takes a cut?

Data purveyors can use these devices in a variety of ways and they often mislead. *Don't you do it!* When you are caught, your integrity is questioned and you have then lost something that has greater worth to you than the total performance of your organization.

Business people do not eagerly seek more data. They are satisfied with what they already have. To attempt to distort information so complicates the use of data that any such effort is self-defeating. No one benefits from creating an illusion that misleads.

9

RESOLVING THE DECISION

. . . .

Applying Actionable Data

You are now at the stage where you and your committee have decided what actionable information is necessary and how and at what level of accuracy and cost it should be obtained. You delay the decision and meet, once again, when all the required information becomes available. Now is the time to apply all your actionable data and resolve the decision, the final stage of the decision-making process.

Let's return once again to the decision on whether or not to market Special Product KR nationally. Your criterion was that if you could sell 500,000 units annually, then you would give the project the go-ahead. Lo and behold, the study you conducted reveals that a sales level of 750,000 is entirely feasible. The next step is easy: Your group quickly decides to proceed with the national roll-out of Special Product KR.

But what if your study uncovers data leading to lower sales projections, say, of 425,000 units annually? Do you then reject Special Project KR and move on to other projects? Yes, if you adhere rigidly to the initial criterion of selling 500,000 units. However, some members of your task force say that, perhaps, some changes can be made to the product, reducing its cost. In that event, an anticipated sales level of 425,000 units would be realistic, and profitable. Still others now argue that the 500,000 figure was too high in the first place, and that the company should go ahead and place the product on the market anyway. A third group may even feel that the study itself was faulty, and the sales prediction of 425,000 units is inaccurate. Further data, they contend, should be gathered before any final action, one way or the other, is taken.

These committee members' suggestions represent a probable "recycling" within the DMP as discussed in Chapter 2. When some of your committee favor altering Special Product KR (so that a 425,000 criterion would be tolerable), they are in essence returning to the formation of alternatives—back to the pre-decisional phase of the decision structure. The same would be true for changing the criterion from 500,000 to 425,000: The group recycles back to the pre-decisional part of the decision structure involving the development of the criteria statement.

The point is that the decision-making process does not necessarily lead to the selection of one alternative once you have gathered the actionable information required by the criterion statement. Decision making is an ongoing and changing process. You can recycle or repeat the same stages again and again until the best possible resolution becomes evident.

Reporting Actionable Data

Suppose you receive actionable survey information that does not quite meet the criterion you stipulated. To return to the same example, anticipated sales of Special Product KR reach only 425,000 rather than 500,000 units. Here, then, is what the KR decision makers *could* do after receiving the actionable data:

1. Market the product nationally

2. Do not market the product nationally

3. Continue the decision delay and gather more information

4. Recycle within the DMP

    (a) Develop new alternatives, e.g. alter the product

    (b) Change the evaluation criterion, e.g. reduce the 500,000 units sales figure to 425,000 units

As the writer of the report you certainly will make a recommendation, suggesting that the decision makers consider one or more of the possibilities. The willingness of the committee to accept such advocacy is to a great extent related to the report writer's ability to communicate. Preparing the report tests one's capacity for artfully and logically organizing and communicating the recommendations to the decision makers. The report is the linchpin of the DMP and, well-prepared, can stir even the "terminally lethargic."

Receiving the report is the point at which the decision makers return to the *mainstream* of the decision structure.

Sequencing the Content of the Report

Chances are good that many times you have written a report with the notion that you must make a tortured attempt to summarize everything on the first page otherwise your boss will not read the thing. This contention has been around for a long time, with understandable but questionable reasons for its support.

No denying that your boss may be busy and has limited time in view of the many demands being made on all sides. But to expect him or her to accept your one-page recommendation for action could in itself have serious profit consequences.

I well recall my having prepared a report on correspondent banks for The Northern Trust Company of Chicago. The issue centered around the extent to which the bank should allocate substantial additional funds to ex-

"Nonsense!"

Source: Drawing by Stevenson; © 1983 The New Yorker Magazine, Inc.

panding its correspondent banking efforts. I was working with Davis Kirby, a vice president, and the report was being presented to Solomon Smith, the bank's chairman. I had hardly started the presentation when Mr. Smith interrupted me with: "Let's turn to the page where you tell us what we should do." Mr. Kirby, with considerable boldness (which I secretly envied), immediately stepped in and cautioned the chairman by saying "Mr. Smith, you *must* take the time to hear the entire report. This is too important a decision for you to rely on only a sentence or two of recommendations!"

Most of us would have wavered in such a situation. But Mr. Kirby hung in there.

When an important course of action is on the line, you cannot buckle and attempt to summarize everything on the first page. If there has been considerable disagreement among the decision makers and if the profit consequences of a wrong decision are high, then *you must build a logical presentation,* following the DMP from beginning to end. To start a report with recommendations is to court disaster. Those who disagreed before the data were obtained will rebel, perhaps with even greater certitude.

Remember, then, that the key to writing an effective report is to organize your thoughts logically. You can use the sequence established by the decision-making process to do this. Remember the five phases through which the decision-making process takes you.

1. Recognize the new environment

2. Develop alternatives

3. Establish evaluation criteria

4. Evaluate alternatives

5. Implement the decision

Your report will be most logical and most persuasive if it follows the same sequence.

The opening of the report should describe the environmental situation that came to the attention of the taskforce at the very outset of the decision structure. Follow this with a discussion (or at least a listing) of the alternatives that were posed during the earlier stages of the decision-making process. The criterion and the reasons for its selection should next be presented, followed by an explanation of the need for new, actionable data, and of how the data were obtained. Next, present the new information, showing how it satisfies or doesn't satisfy the criterion. Finally, state your recommendation on what the organization should do next. If you have argued your case well and have presented it logically, the best recommendation should emerge naturally from your report.

In this way, the entire picture, leading up to the selection of one alternative over others is presented. As you develop each phase of the DMP, you lead the readers along a well-grounded path so that later they cannot argue with what you say. You point out that there was agreement on the stated decisional options. You stress the complete acceptance of the criteria on which the selection of an alternative was based. You present the actionable data, demonstrating how the information satisfies—or does not satisfy—the criteria. Then you state the obvious: the recommended course of action that emerges from the data.

As you prepare your report, pay particular attention to those aspects of the decision-making process that evoked the most discussion or the highest levels of disagreement in earlier meetings. The decision makers are likely to return to these points before deciding on any course of action. Let's assume, for example, that the formulation of alternatives had earlier resulted in heated discussions. As report writer, you must take care to detail the reasoning that went into the selection of the final list of options, showing all those alternatives that were considered but which, for reasons you describe in your report, did not make it to the final list. In this way, by

incorporating—and dismissing—issues on which the decision makers earlier disagreed, you can avoid the possibility that a member of the group
will want to revitalize those issues.

I remember a midwestern regional brewery client that for years had a
highly successful logo. The firm's management had decided, however, to
change to a new label, and the marketing research firm with which I was
associated was engaged to determine which of two labels developed by industrial designers should be adopted. The data were clear enough, and I
presented the findings to the brewery management. After I recommended
one label over the other, based on the procured actionable data, the company's chairman spoke up, protesting ''But you haven't told us whether we
even *need* a new label!'' The chairman had not attended the earlier meetings
during which the Label A and Label B alternatives were agreed upon as the
two finalists. *Whether* a new label was needed was no longer an issue. That a
new label was needed had *already* been resolved. But the chairman's statement had the effect of saying that the survey was light years off the real issue. It was as though the chairman had handed me a lighted firecracker.
You can be sure the management team left me there to twist in the wind, for
no member was about to counter the chairman's comment.

I had erred in my report. I should have explained that the issue of
whether to adopt a new label had already been resolved and that the management had agreed to the two alternative labels to be studied.

Arithmetic is no substitute for judgment, but with a report that follows
the sequence and flow of the DMP you can expect success in your effort to
persuade the decision makers to accept your recommendations.

Of course, presenting a well-written report is no guarantee that your
recommendations will be accepted. Your fellow decision makers may disagree with any aspect of your arguments, from choice of alternatives or
criteria, to the accuracy or relevance of new data. However, by sequencing your report according to the decision-making process you have followed, you will be able to prepare yourself for any questions, comments,
or objections that arise.

So, having submitted your report to the decision makers (or, having
received the report) you have participated in the making of the final decision. The data contained in the report have reduced the decision makers'
disagreement, a recommendation was made, and one of the options under
consideration was adopted, based on the criterion already agreed upon.

A decision has been made. Now what happens? The final chapter
takes us beyond the decision.

10

BEYOND THE DECISION

As every reader of this book knows by now, decision making is an on-going cyclical activity, central to business operations. The making of any decision—major or minor, tactical or strategic, monetary or non-monetary—creates a new environment for future decision making.

The specific nature of this new setting cannot be predicted with any degree of certainty. The best we can do is make sure we are prepared. This is why it is important that analyzing environments does not stop once the decision is made. Beyond the decision, we must plan for possible future moves.

• •

Post-Decisional Planning

At the beginning of the book, we identified three types of new environments that can influence our success or failure: the Threat, the Deviation from the Expected, and the Lurking Situation that can offer new opportunities for change. Let's now look at post-decisional planning in terms of these three environments.

Back to our standby example, Special Product KR. You just made the decision to market the item. But this doesn't mean you can just sit back with a smile on your face and relax. There's still a lot more work to do.

The first step is to monitor the new environment your decision has created. And to monitor it successfully, you must consider how it might be affected by all three types of environmental change.

First, the Threat. How might the competition react to your introduction of Special Product KR onto the market, especially if it develops into a highly successful item in your line? There are several plans you can make to help you anticipate and respond to competitive reactions. You can alert your sales staff to be on the look-out for any counter-moves that might be initiated by the competition. Work out your next move in advance, well before competitors take action. This is where business moves come to resemble military moves—you have to predict and plan for the enemy's response to your every maneuver. What if your competition were to introduce a similar product? Plan ahead and obtain consumer reaction to a couple of new features that might feasibly be added to Special Product KR to differentiate it from anticipated me-too products. Or, what if your competition were to place a competing item on the market at a substantially reduced price? To prepare for this eventuality, you could test the sales of Special Product KR at varying price levels, and will then be able to respond immediately to a competitive price confrontation. In short, be prepared for threats. Stay one step ahead of the competition, so that whatever move they make, you can fight back.

Second, the Deviation from the Expected. What happens if Special Product KR does not perform as you expected when you made the decision to market it nationally? Perhaps, for example, it gains a sales level well in excess of forecasts, or perhaps sales are disappointing, at a level well below your predictions. Careful monitoring of sales will help you prepare for either eventuality. Some informal measurement of overall customer satisfaction, related to specific likes and dislikes, could reveal data that would aid you in adjusting the product or your marketing efforts to respond to unexpected situations. Is a pricing change a possibility? Would a shift in the basic copy theme of the advertising be in order? Watch your sales carefully and make comparisons with your original forecasts so that you notice immediately if things begin to go off track. Then, take remedial action.

Third, the Lurking Situation. This is where good planning can offer the greatest opportunities for creativity in the post-decisional stage. By monitoring the effects of your decision—in this example, the introduction of Special Product KR nationally—you can uncover new information that will pave the way for new ideas and opportunities.

A case example: post-decisional planning at Coca Cola

In 1990 Coca-Cola began a unique sales promotion scheme. The company developed a can that looked similar, if not identical to, a regular Coca-Cola Classic can, but which contained instead of the soft drink, money—five dollar bills—and certificates for prizes. These MagiCans, as they were named, were randomly distributed with other Coca-Cola Classic cans to retail outlets, ready to be purchased by the lucky winners.

Supported by a $100 million advertising campaign, the MagiCans were introduced with great fanfare during the early summer of 1990.

To Coca-Cola's dismay, a minute number of the cans malfunctioned during the early stages of the promotion. Several dozen consumers complained at the outset that the prize-delivering mechanisms inside the MagiCans were broken, and in one case a boy was reported to have consumed the ''foul-smelling'' liquid within the can (but with no ill effects). Only three weeks into the campaign, the Coca-Cola management became so concerned that the malfunction might damage the company's image that it called off the MagiCan promotion, leaving the company with undistributed MagiCans numbering well into six digits. This presented a new issue: What to do with the cans? Coca-Cola had, in its official rules, stated that a given number of MagiCans would yield designated prizes: some 560,050 cans would each pop open with a $5 bill.

A Deviation from the Expected, then, made Coca-Cola decide to pull the MagiCan campaign. The malfunction—and the public's reaction to it—was totally unpredicted and the results were extremely damaging. How should the company adjust to this new situation? The company had monitored the progress of the promotional campaign and discovered the malfunction as early as possible. A quick management decision was made to call off the campaign. But the company did not stop there. Consumer research was immediately launched to measure the extent of damage—if any—to the brand's image. New alternatives were formulated. What marketing effort would replace the Classic MagiCan promotion? What would happen to the unused MagiCans? (Reintroducing the MagiCan at a later date certainly had to be one of the options.) In brief, what could be done to get the situation under control and return to normal? By carefully monitoring the effects of the decision to use MagiCans in a promotion, and by planning for the unexpected, Coca-Cola managed to minimize its losses and avert possible disastrous effects on corporate image.

. . . .

Communicating with Non-Decision Makers

We began this book by talking about people and their importance in the decision-making process. Let's close the book in the same way.

People are at the center of any decision. Without them, decisions— and the progress and opportunities they bring—are impossible. It stands to reason, then, that being a good decision maker is all about understanding and communicating well with others. In the post-decision phase, too, people are important. Plans move forward more smoothly and monitoring performance is an easier task when people cooperate well with one another.

Let's take a simple, everyday situation to illustrate this point. Nothing seems more exasperating than to walk up to a counter in a department store and have to wait what seems an endless amount of time for the attention of a clerk who is busily engaged in adding up a column of figures, or chatting to a co-worker. If only the clerk would communicate with us, we would feel much better about having to wait. A quick nod and a smile would go a long way in easing our frustration. There is something about our egos that makes us crave attention from others.

When making plans that involve others, makes sure you pave the way by playing up to their egos. For your plans to go smoothly, you need the cooperation of people outside the decision-making team. Acknowledge their contributions by letting them know as early as possible what is going to happen and how they will be involved. Get everyone into the act. This is the best way of winning cooperation when the time comes. It also assures those surrounding the decision-making activity that they are important enough to be kept informed on what is happening. It not only appeals to their egos; it encourages their support. Like the clerk who nods and smiles at customers awaiting service, keeping your people informed is the groundwork for a good working relationship.

How far up and down the organizational ladder this communication effort should be dispersed depends, of course, on the nature of the decision. A broad tactical decision that implements a basic corporate policy would certainly require widespread communication. In contrast, obviously, for actions that affect a narrower segment of the organization, more specialized communications and information networks would work. In any event, keeping others informed is essential to optimum implementation of decisions.

Monitoring the post-decisional environment requires continuous effort. It can be the beginning of one or many more new decision structures. Don't wait for information to come to you. Go after it. In every business day and in every business activity, watch for signs of change or opportunities for progress and make the most of them. Creative ideas emerge. Alternatives dawn. New decisions are on their way that will paint a new picture for the future of your organization.

Decision making is always.

APPENDIX: LOGIC DIAGRAM

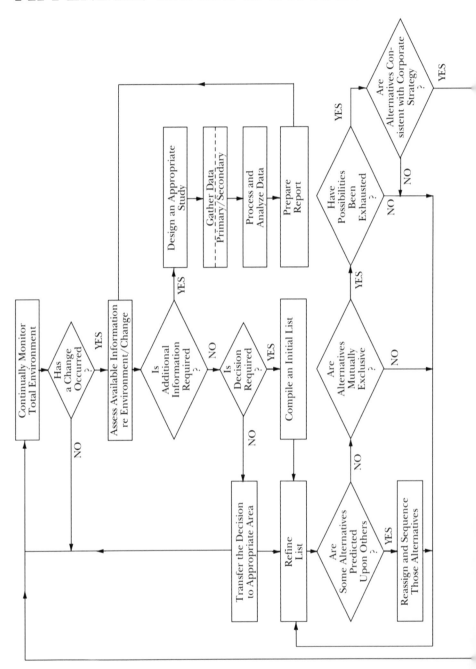

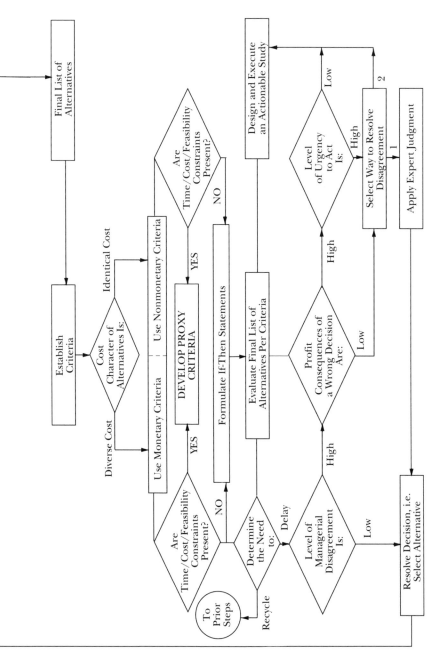

Adapted with permission, from *Marketing Decision Making*, O'Dell, *et al*, First Edition, South-Western Publishing Co., Cincinnati, 1976

INDEX